Praise for *Trust by Design*

"We want others to trust us. We want to enjoy relationships based on trust. And we need institutions that are worthy of our trust. Amy Valdez Barker names the erosion of trust in our culture and at the same time grounds our desire for trust, and our calling to be trustworthy, in the nature and gifts of God. This wonderful resource will help us examine ourselves and lead more faithfully in this complicated season."
—Ken Carter, Resident Bishop, Florida Area, The United Methodist Church

"*Trust by Design* offers both a remarkably comprehensive and stunningly simple diagnosis of our world: at the core of its brokenness is a lack of trust. Amy Valdez Barker reminds us that rebuilding that trust in our relationships, churches, and communities is the critical mission of our time. Doing so is not easy, but this book points the way."
—Magrey R. deVega, Senior Pastor, Hyde Park United Methodist Church, Tampa, FL

"In a world where trust is eroding rapidly in government, institutions, and even the church, Dr. Barker bravely names a way forward. Our ability to trust God's goodness and grace is tempered by our relationships with others! Through dynamic scholarship, deep biblical reflection, honest sharing, and practical advice, she supports the Christian calling to trust God and also restore trust in one another. Amy's faith shines through every page as she offers leaders practical ideas on how to rebuild trust for the sake of the church's mission. We recommend this 'must read' for anyone who is in ministry or is part of a faith community today."
—Terence Corkin and Julia Kuhn Wallace, authors of *The Church Guide to Making Decisions Together* and the blog makingchurchdecisions.com

"Amy Valdez Barker is heartsick. She's mystified and impatient. Humble, inquisitive, and insightful, she's also expectant and confident. Amy's sure that we want to and ought to do better—to be better. What's holding us back?

In the pages of *Trust by Design*, Valdez Barker is on a mission. She invites us to adopt a deep yearning and genuine hope as we apply straightforward methods to build layers of trust—the kind of trust that reinvigorates our vision, emboldens our aspirations, enriches our relationships, and helps shape loving and just places to work and live.

Cogently illuminating the interplay of theological, psychological, and sociological elements, she presents a blueprint that helps us visualize our own capacity to reimagine, reclaim, and radiate trust. Step-by-step we participate in a persuasive and nuanced examination of more than a cliché. We affirm the power and necessity of trust, repent of the practices that degrade it, and discover surefooted pathways for building and sustaining the underpinnings of rich and rewarding collaboration and friendships.

Trust by Design is not a volume for your shelf; it's a thoughtful, insightful, accessible, and convincing roadmap that can lead you—and all of us—to do something wonderful."

—Neil M. Alexander, President and Publisher Emeritus, United Methodist Publishing House

AMY VALDEZ BARKER
With Foreword by Kenda Creasy Dean

TRUST
BY DESIGN

The Beautiful Behaviors
of an Effective Church Culture

 Abingdon Press
Nashville

TRUST BY DESIGN:
THE BEAUTIFUL BEHAVIORS OF AN EFFECTIVE CHURCH CULTURE

Copyright © 2017 by Abingdon Press

All rights reserved.

Library of Congress Cataloging-in-Publication Data has been requested.

ISBN: 978-1-5018-4244-3

17 18 19 20 21 22 23 24 25 26—10 9 8 7 6 5 4 3 2 1

MANUFACTURED IN THE UNITED STATES OF AMERICA

The Church: Trust Training Centers

This book helps leaders explore the interconnections of building trust in our communities of faith. As church leaders prepare meetings, conferences, and small group gatherings, and are seeking to create environments that foster and facilitate a high-trust culture, there are a few practices to keep in mind. Consider these five practices as you prepare your gatherings in your community of faith.

1. Create a space that is open, hospitable, welcoming, and safe. People are much more open to trusting when you have taken time to consider their safety, security, and needs in the environment in which they will gather.

2. Be committed to being a leader/facilitator who is willing to really listen. People will trust you and trust the group when they believe that you aren't trying to fix, advise, correct, or "save" them. As people of faith, we have to establish God as the ultimate creator and judge.

3. Do your best to ask honest, open questions that allow the group to "hear each other into speech." When people feel free to wrestle with questions together, there is a gift of discovering more because we trust one another to explore a multitude of ideas. Creative ideas and innovation can be messy. Let them be messy, and follow God through the refining process.

4. Explore the intersection of the universal stories of human experience with the personal stories of our lives in relation to the scriptures and our understanding of God. Let theology be intertwined in your gathering. Looking at ideas and stories through a theological lens helps us trust God as we learn to trust our neighbors.

5. Adult learning needs multiple modes of exploration and reflection. Keep in mind what ways people might digest information, wrestle with questions, and understand their role and responsibility as they engage one another in this community.[1]

---

1. These ideas are adapted from Parker Palmer's "Circles of Trust." It is explored in detail in chapter 5 of this book.

Contents

Contents

Foreword

I can't think of a more urgent discussion for the church to have right now than the one this book proposes. Is trust an idea whose time has come—or a virtue so quaint that not even Christians can utter the word without an eye-roll of irony?

In a culture where the Oxford Dictionary made *post-truth* the 2016 Word of the Year and "alternative facts" are issued from the White House, it is little wonder that trust is having a time of it. The word *trust* comes from a word that the Saxons spelled *treowe*, or true, faithful. In old-fashioned wedding ceremonies, the couple pledged one another their "troth"—to be true or have fidelity to one another. To trust people means to have confidence in them, to rely on their integrity, their steadfastness; they are trustworthy. Our wordy, brain-oriented culture has often turned faith into a head trip, and somewhere along the way "believing" in Christ turned into a checklist of "beliefs" *about* God, wresting faith from its origins in trust. But when Jesus told his followers, "Believe in me," what he meant was: "Trust me. Have confidence in me. I am trustworthy. You can rely on me because I am faithful."

Did you catch that? Jesus wasn't asking his *followers* to be faithful; he was saying he is faithful to *them*. Jesus didn't focus on trust. He focused on being trustworthy.

It's just the kind of upside-down logic we should have learned by now to expect from Jesus, except that we forget about it, every single time. And because we forget about it, our churches, like our country, are mired in the mud of massive games of intra-nicene chicken. Who will blink first? Who will be the first to dig ourselves out of the morasses we have dug for ourselves after decades of embarrassing Jesus, missing the bigger picture, arguing over nonessentials that divide us, as flock after flock throw up their hooves in disgust and wander off in search of greener pastures?

Levels of trust in the United States are cause for concern. Maybe we shouldn't have been surprised by the 2016 election and the historically low levels of trust carried by both parties' presidential nominees. Fewer than a third of Americans think other people are trustworthy (make that only 19 percent if you're a young adult).[1] American public trust in government, information, and even in the public's potential wisdom are at historic lows.[2] The American Psychological Association's 2014 Work and Well-Being Survey found that one in four American workers don't trust their employers, and only half think their employers are "honest and upfront" with them.[3] The massive Edelman Trust Barometer—which measures global trust in non-governmental organizations, government, media, and business—revealed the largest ever drop in trust across all four institutions in 2017. Trust in media was at an all-time low in most countries, and government was the least trusted institution in half of the countries surveyed. CEO credibility plummeted to an all-time low in every country surveyed, with government leaders being the least credible of all. "The implications of the global trust crisis are deep and wide-ranging," the report concludes.

---

1. Pew Research Center, "Millennials Less Trusting of Others," March 5, 2014, http://www.pewsocialtrends.org/2014/03/07/millennials-in-adulthood/sdt-next-america-03-07-2014-0-05/.

2. Lee Rainie, "The New Landsape of Facts and Trust," Pew Research Center (Internet and Technology), April 21, 2017, http://www.pewinternet.org/2017/04/21/the-new-landscape-of-facts-and-trust/.

3. "Employee Distrust Pervasive in American Workforce," American Psychological Association, April 23, 2014, http://www.apa.org/news/press/releases/2014/04/employee-distrust.aspx.

"The consequence is virulent populism and nationalism as the mass population has taken control away from the elites."[4] Of the four institutions, only business is viewed as potentially making a difference, *if* it increases profits *and* improves economic and social conditions in the communities where it operates.[5]

The founding fathers and mothers built skepticism into our institutions—including churches—for good reasons. Sin is real, and checks and balances have proven to be good ways to keep human nature in check. And yet, go figure: Things may not be as hopeless as they seem. We may have lost trust in institutions, but statistics notwithstanding, we seem perennially hopeful about trusting *people*. According to the Pew Charitable Trust, if you are an active Facebook user, you are three times more likely than a non-Internet user to believe that most people are trustworthy. You probably placed an order online sometime in the past month, which means you entrusted your credit card information to someone you don't know, who received the transaction. Trust seems to be somewhat correlated with other variables, like hope and an external locus of control. People who think the world is getting better and who feel in control of their circumstances are more likely to make a choice to trust others and to teach their children to do the same (see figure 1).[6]

---

4. Robert Edelman, "2017 Edelman Trust Barometer Reveals Global Implosion of Trust," January 15, 2017, http://www.edelman.com/news/2017-edelman -trust-barometer-reveals-global-implosion/. The study notes that people now view media as part of the elite: "A person like yourself (60%) is now just as credible a source of information about a company as is a technical (60%) or academic (60%) expert, and far more credible than a CEO (37%) and government official (29%)."

5. Ibid.

6. Also see Charles Green, interviewed by Jacob Morgan, "Trust and the Future of Work," *Forbes,* September 11, 2014, https://www.forbes.com/sites/jacob morgan/2014/09/11/trust-in-the-workplace-what-happened-to-it-and-how-do -we-get-it-back/#1d373aca7030; and Robert F. Hurley, "The Decision to Trust," *Harvard Business Review,* September 2006, https://hbr.org/2006/09/the-decision -to-trust.

FIGURE 1

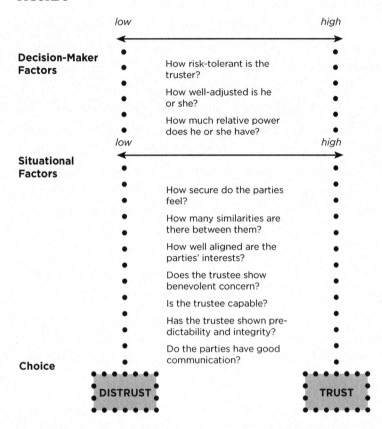

Meanwhile, the "trust economy" is booming.[7] We allow complete strangers to rent our extra bedrooms, drive us to the dentist, run errands, dogsit our Saint Bernard, and take us to dinner in a foreign country. AirBnB rentals outstrip hotel rentals three to one in Tokyo;[8] New

---

7. Cf. Rachel Botsman, "The Currency of the New Economy Is Trust," TED Talk, June 2012, https://www.ted.com/talks/rachel_botsman_the_currency_of_the_new_economy_is_trust.

8. Deanna Ting, "6 Takeaways about AirBnB's Potential Impact on the Hotel Industry," *Skift*, January 23, 2017, https://skift.com/2017/01/23/6-takeaways-about-airbnbs-potential-impact-on-the-hotel-industry/.

York now has more Uber drivers than yellow taxis;[9] TaskRabbit will assemble your IKEA mess in no time flat (assembling IKEA furniture is reportedly TaskRabbit's most common request); Rover sends "Melissa" to dogsit your pooch (you've never met "Melissa," but the website reviews describe her as "the dog-whisperer," so you feel pretty good about the arrangement); and when you visit Paris, you sign up on VoulezVous-Diner to have a meal at a local Parisian's home, who cooks local fare for you. And that doesn't include the Broadway tickets you bought on eBay to *Hello, Dolly*, which cost a fortune, but you trust the seller to send them. After all, if he doesn't, you'll leave him terrible feedback online, which would ruin his four-star online reputation.

On the surface, it looks like the surveys are right—business seems to be the last bastion of trust left, since all of these examples are businesses. Yet these examples illustrate something else as well: relationships. It's not business that makes the "trust economy" work; it's *relationships*—and relationships are the backbone of every institution, starting with the church. Our confidence in institutions depends upon these entities' ability to connect to us relationally, which makes the following data set emblematic of a larger problem facing congregations. Regardless of whether they regularly attend church or not, the piece of information that most millennials (82%) will share with a church is their first name. Remember, this age group leaves their e-mails and personal information online for any number of consumer items daily. In addition:

- 53% give their last names

- 33% share their e-mail address

- 19% share their physical address

- 12% share their phone number

9. Brett Helling and Syed Ajmal, accessed May 28, 2017, https://rideshare apps.com/2015-rideshare-infographic/.

- 6% share social media information

- 15% don't share *anything* at all (among non-Christians, 28%)[10]

What's going on here? I think the issue is rather straightforward. The church asks a lot in terms of trust *from* people. We just don't demonstrate very much of it. Yet if Jesus was right about this, we have the prior responsibility. First, we must be worthy of trust. Then perhaps someone will trust us. First, we must be faithful to others, and then maybe someone will find reason to be faithful to the church. That's the nature of grace. God's hand is always extended first.

In her Gifford Lectures (and, more briefly, in her TED talk), Cambridge University philosophy professor Baronness Onora O'Neill makes this very point. Speaking from the perspective of an ethicist, Professor O'Neill argues that aiming to have more trust—as a church or as a society—is missing the point. After all, you want more trust in the competent, the reliable, and the honest, but what about the incompetent? The unreliable? The dishonest? Maybe not. No, she says, we should aim for *trustworthiness*—but even this is its own hot mess. Every time we construct a system for greater accountability, to build greater trustworthiness, it just gets in the way. Consider the midwife who told O'Neill it was taking longer to do the paperwork than to deliver the baby. Trust, in the end, she says, can't be built—it must be given. Other people give it to you. All you can do is construct the basis on which people give it to you. You have to *be trustworthy*. You have to provide usable evidence that you are faithful. How? Every day, by making yourself vulnerable and reliable to the other person.[11]

---

10. "What Millennials Want When They Visit Church," March 4, 2015, https://www.barna.org/barna-update/millennials/711-what-millennials-want-when-they-visit-church#.VdtlqnsmxUN.

11. Onora O'Neill, "Autonomy and Trust in Bioethics," The Gifford Lectures, University of Edinburgh (2000–2001); also TED Talk, "What We Don't Understand about Trust," September 13, 2013, https://www.youtube.com/watch?v=1PNX6M_dVsk.

Given the crisis of trust of our culture and our church, this book has reached us in the nick of time. In the pages ahead, Dr. Amy Valdez Barker describes ways in which Christian people can become more vulnerable and reliable to one another and to the communities we serve. She not only offers an analysis of what happens when distrust arises in church, she also explores, in depth, our theological responses as people who belong to God and to each other. Finally, she offers practical disciplines that help us rebuild foundations for trustworthiness, ways that we can practice vulnerability to God and to each other, becoming more reliable and steadfast in our work together as people of faith.

The thing is, Jesus has already demonstrated the way. He didn't set out to build trust. He set out to *be* trustworthy, to have "troth," to be vulnerable to the point of death, to be utterly true to us. Not only did God become, in Christ, the ultimate example of trustworthiness, but God, in Christ, became trustworthy on our behalf. Jesus already knows we are not going to get this right. That should not stop us from trying, but to be trustworthy for one another—to be vulnerable and reliable and faithful and true—is a daunting, lifelong, beg-forgiveness, start-over, try-again task that the stuff of being human is made of.

Maybe let's let Jesus go first.

Kenda Creasy Dean
Ocean Grove, NJ

Preface

I've always thought that authors of books represented expertise in the topic that they are writing about. But it would be a dangerous endeavor to think that I could ever offer expertise in trust, especially Christian trust. Authors are supposed to be those who exemplify that topic, that area of interest, right? I mean, look at fitness books, cookbooks, self-help books, and leadership books. These are authors who seem to have it all together, who have figured out a way to perfect those skills and ideas, and then they have taken on the role of teaching those skills to others. Well, if that's what you're looking for, this isn't that kind of book. I am no expert on trust. I don't proclaim to have mastered the skill and ability of building trust, nor do I proclaim to be the most trustworthy person. I am, however, very interested in "wondering out loud" about topics of the human soul. I am interested in exploring the depths of virtues and values that contribute to the Christian journey. I am fascinated by the intersections of theology, psychology, and sociology. I want to test concepts and wander around God's creation discovering how God is at work in our world through our relationships with one another and our explorations for our own inner souls. Trust is one of those less chartered territories that I was interested in exploring as my own experience in community around the matters of trust were disrupted by my own thinking and the behaviors of leaders in my denomination. Hence, this book on trust is a theological, sociological, and psychological exploration of God's intention for me, my church, and the community where I live. I hope you'll join me on this exploration and discover something new that helps you on your journey through faith.

Acknowledgments

A s my first published book, outside of my dissertation, I want to thank my family, Rich, Ashtin, and Tré for trusting me to get this done without completely disrupting our lives. And I want to thank Margaret Ann Crain and Kenda Creasy Dean for being partners in this endeavor and helping me find my voice and share it with others.

Introduction

I stood at the edge of the concrete table surrounded by the weeping willows, draped with Spanish moss. I crossed my arms and held my breath as I looked skyward and prayed to God that the group of small seventh and eighth graders would catch my body as I let go of my inhibitions and let my body fall backward. Every single one of those twenty middle schoolers had already done this before, and as their youth director, I was the last one to go. I thought I could get out of it as the adult in the group. It's one thing to let these kids catch each other with adults sprinkled in between. It's a whole other thing to let them catch me, the full-grown woman who was a bit self-conscious about my weight and definitely a little less trusting because of life experiences. Why did it matter so much that I join these middle schoolers in taking the leap of faith and participating in the trust fall, as they did? Because it was needed. It was needed for me and it was necessary for them to see that I trusted them just as much as they trusted me. Faith communities, including youth groups, are places where we learn to practice trust, live as trustworthy people, and model trust for a trust-deficient world.

Several years later I remembered that experience with the youth group when a consultant asked our planning team, "In an organization whose fundamental principles are built upon trust, why wouldn't you trust the information being reported?" This questioned disturbed me while I sat there doubting the numbers in the in-depth research report on church worship attendance. I realized that she was right! We should trust the numbers reported by clergy because we expect spiritual leaders to be honest and trustworthy. It's what we preach and what we teach as we invite people to trust God and trust each other. So why were so many people doubting the numbers, questioning the accuracy of the data, and wondering whether or not clergy are truly trustworthy? Could it be that trust gets complicated by nuances and layers of fact? Or that methods of data collection are faulty? Or that clergy fall to the human need to be perceived as successful too? What might be giving leaders the urge to justify small adjustments in numbers?

I wanted to believe that the data reported about worship attendance was trustworthy. However, having served in congregations and watched colleagues nonchalantly fill out the end-of-year forms without meticulous records or accurate counts of people in worship, I didn't trust the data. Why does that matter? In our system, the numbers matter because they determine several decisions that affect people's lives in a congregation. The number of people in worship determines the number of bishops appointed to a particular area in our connection. The number of people in worship is used to calculate the number of dollars apportioned to each regional annual conference so that other ministries in the connection are funded. The number of members in a particular area is also used to calculate the number of delegates that represent a particular region in the church. Even in government organizations, numbers determine financial support, leaders deployed to an area, and estimated resources distributed to a particular area. For example, in several countries in Europe, the number of people in a denomination is tied to the amount of currency given to that institution by the government throughout the year. These numbers matter in so many of our systems, so if we can't trust our leadership to report accurate numbers, can we trust their decisions and their leadership? On the other side of the conversation, it made me wonder what else is going on with the clergy leadership in the church. Were they afraid that the numbers would somehow be used against them? Were they concerned that the denominational leaders would punish them if the numbers were not favorable?

Did they trust the leaders who were using the numbers to dig deeper and ask the right questions to better understand their circumstances? If not, why not? Trust is a fundamental principle in any organization.

But trust isn't fundamental merely because of the logistical and administrative aspects of our work. Trust is fundamental because it implicates our spiritual brand and our ministry product. Our ministry product depends on faith (which is a theological synonym in the New Testament for trust). Our spiritual brand is built on the foundation of trust in God and trust in those who share our Christian endeavor. This is why leaders spend so much time in children's ministry programs and youth ministry programs to teach them how to trust. Almost every youth ministry group I have been a part of and have led, created activities that teach trust. From "trust falls," to "rope courses," to "circles of trust," church leaders seek ways to teach children and youth techniques that build trust.[1]

One of these trust-building activities was at a ropes course in the north Georgia woods. A young man, nearly a foot and a half taller than me, and I had to cross two parallel ropes suspended fifty feet above the ground. The only way we could get across was to trust each other by locking hands and slowly inching our way across the ropes, leaning on one another, to hold each other up. If one pushed too hard, the other would lose balance and fall. If one didn't push hard enough, we would both come crashing to the "metaphorical ground." Together, we had to find just the right balance to make our way across the rope. The five-minute exercise felt as though it took an eternity, and more than a couple expletives were on the tip of this fifteen-year-old's tongue. As we were about halfway across, he looked me in the eyes and said, "Ms. Amy,

---

1. Erik Erikson's psycho-social development timeline illustrates how the development of trust is fundamental at the early stages of life. An infant who successfully navigates this first stage of life has a greater chance of developing a sense of security, value, and self-worth. Educators have understood how critical this stage of development is for identity formation. Because of this, there has been greater emphasis on partnering with parents, educators, doctors, and even church leaders in equipping adults in their generative role in nurturing children through these stages of development.

if you weren't a pastor right now, I'd be saying something different." I took a deep breath and said, "Jay,[2] if you weren't a youth right now, I might be saying something different too!" He laughed and we both nearly lost our balance, but it helped us get past the halfway point and we learned how to trust each other's willingness and abilities in order to make it to the other side. It was an exercise in trust that strengthened the relationship between leader and student, which carried us through to his graduation.

---

2. Name changed to protect identity.

Why Trust?

The Trust Deficit

Unfortunately, the lack of trust across our nations, our cultures, and our communities is palpable. Consider a troubling election year where millions of people around the world witnessed a dangerous collapse of trust in government leaders. Across Europe, Australia, and Asia, governments have called for resignations of their heads of state, presidents have resigned before their terms have ended, and political leaders are being questioned. In the United States alone, there has been a rise of concern around the public conversations about "alternative facts" and questions about the integrity of the media's responsibility for shedding light on subjective information. When the leaders of the nation proclaim a complete lack of trust in the very institutions charged with keeping the public informed, we can begin to see the tears in the cultural tapestry of the fabric of trust. Consider the journalists in Boston who exposed the Catholic Church's lack of transparency for decades concerning child abuse. Racial, tribal, and religious tensions appear to be (once again) dangerously high in places all around the world. An October 2016 Pew Research Study survey in the United States indicates that Americans trust the military more than they trust the church.[1]

---

1. Brian Kennedy, "Most Americans Trust the Military and Scientists to Act in the Public's Interest," Pew Research Center, October 18, 2016, http://www.pew research.org/fact-tank/2016/10/18/most-americans-trust-the-military-and -scientists-to-act-in-the-publics-interest/.

Everywhere we turn we are reminded of the profound fissures along the lines of gender, race and class, just to name a few. The truth is these fissures and divisions are not new and not directly attributable to the long campaign season just ended. For many years, there has been a growing trust deficit in public leadership and institutions. These are trying times, and the fabric of who we are and who we aspire to be has been stretched beyond anything we desire to look upon. But look upon it squarely we must.[2]

The faith-based institutions in our world are integral to the soul of humanity. As Christians, we worship a God who constantly asks us to put our trust in Jesus, whose life, death, and resurrection give us hope for the fullness of life in this world. Nicky Gumbel, lead pastor at Harvest Bible Church in London, writes in his daily devotional, "Faith, in the Bible, is primarily about putting our trust in a person. In that sense it is more akin to love. All loving relationships involve some element of trust. Faith is trust in God that transforms all our other relationships."[3] The church institution, government institutions, schools, and hospitals are created and designed because we believe in human flourishing and we believe that in order to flourish, people need to work together, support one another, and ultimately trust one another so that people can survive, live, and thrive. Whether we call it love or not, for Christians it is about loving our neighbors, and if we are to live out this faith principle, we must trust our neighbors so that they can trust us and ultimately come to discover the gifts from trusting God.

Therefore, perceptions about trust in our faith-based institutions must change. This book invites you to look at the fissures and step into the gaps as Christians who lead in churches, in schools, in hospitals, in government institutions, in businesses, and in communities throughout

---

2. Bishop Gregory Palmer, "Pastoral Letter Written to the West Ohio Annual Conference," NewsNet, a West Ohio Conference digital publication, November 9, 2016, http://conta.cc/2oDYDes.

3. Nicky Gumbel, *Bible in One Year 2017*, accessed April 4, 2017, https://www.bibleinoneyear.org/.

the world. Christ invites us to live worthy of Christ's trust in us as we put our whole trust in his love and grace.

In this book, we will explore the design of faith-based systems that are intended to build trust and connect us with a creator whose great love for humanity is experienced through our love of one another. As leaders in the church, trust is a sacred asset that must be carefully handled with deep respect and priceless value. As leaders, we strive toward a complete Christian maturity that offers the world a vision of Christ here and now. We want people to discover the gift of our trustworthy Savior through our own lived witness and our own trust in Christ. But it isn't solely in our hands; mutual trust is the gift of the Holy Spirit who uses our faithfulness to reach all of God's creation. When we put our whole trust in Christ and live and act as trustworthy leaders, our lives are evidence of God's beautiful work through the dearly loved Christian community because of God's love for us.

Why I Care—And You Should Too!

Ironically, I started out pursuing this book project because I was responding to a colleague's interest on the topic of trust. He thought this would be the kind of thing the church should be talking about. And at first, I began pursuing the topic because I felt this was an idea I introduced and I was afraid that he would take my idea and turn it into a book. In other words, I didn't trust him. But the more I explored this idea, the more it challenged me and then convicted me as a leader in my church.

I am seeing more of the divisions in our society, in our popular culture, and in the US political landscape. Tremors of change are happening throughout the world, which are evidence of seismic shifts that are eroding our mutual trust. Fundamental human values are challenged. In some cases the church is speaking out against abuses and in many cases the church has been silent.

In the business world, trust is receiving much attention from authors such as Charles Feltman, author of *The Thin Book of Trust*.[4] Though the business world is recognizing a deficit of trust, very few resources are available from religious perspectives, which is surprising, because trust is a core feature of our Christian identity. I've discovered that people don't trust people who want to talk about trust, even if it comes from a place of curiosity and wonder, rather than from judgment and fear.

But the business world isn't the only world that needs to be talking about trust. Church leaders and participants in the Christian faith need to be openly and honestly exploring what we mean by trust. We need to figure out if we are striving toward the same outcomes when we talk about trusting one another. And we need to wrestle with what we mean by "trusting God."

Does our trust in God translate to trust in neighbor? Should it? If we can't trust our neighbors or our leaders (in the church and elsewhere), then what makes us think that we can really trust God?

Rachel Botsman points to a great disruption in our understanding and our use of trust. On technology platforms and through information exchange in social media or with massive databases, we are willing to trust strangers more than institutions because of the "reputation banks" that technology is creating. How does this affect the way we see each other, engage with one another, and even understand faith through a shifting digital, cultural landscape?

The church should wrestle with these shifts in the culture, in part because of the implications for trust in God, trust in Christ, and trust in our faith communities. In this exploration we look at the world through social and cultural contexts, we look at the scriptures, and we seek the threads of trust that are necessary in a community for people to live together and experience human flourishing for all.

---

4. Charles Feltman, *The Thin Book of Trust: An Essential Primer for Building Trust at Work* (Bend, OR: Thin Book Publishing Co, 2009), 1.

Trust by Design

A friend and I were about to walk down the stairs into the Modern American art display at the Crystal Bridges Art Museum in Little Rock, Arkansas. A couple stood at the bottom of the stairs looking up. We started down the stairs and then looked up. We saw this beautiful art installation constructed by millions and millions of long, thin strings stretched across hundreds of tiny hooks. As we looked at the art and changed the direction of our gaze, the image changed. If we stood in one corner, we saw a different color blend. If we stood under the center of the design, we saw a soft red-orange color blend; and if we walked past the design, we discovered a blue-purple color blend. It wasn't a woven cloth, but the strings were carefully placed together to create this optical brilliance. There were several layers and yet it looked like one seamless piece. Gabriel Dawes, the designer, painstakingly connected each string, knowing how they would work together to strengthen one another's characteristics and come together to show the observer something beautiful, something breathtaking, something that left you wondering, hope-filled and in love with the creation. It was a beautiful design.

Imagine God's creation as a harmonious and complex design. God wants people to see what God can create when we discover the elements that God planted within us to weave together a beautiful design of people working together, trusting one another to bring about systems that are designed for human flourishing. Trust is the design that God gives us to discover our interwoven nature, which brings about goodness, peace, and possibility in the world. Through our trust-filled, trustworthy actions, attitudes, and behaviors, we strengthen our faith in God and faith in each other. We strengthen our hope for the world, hope for creation, hope for the beloved body of Christ. And we strengthen and confirm the love God has for us and the love we have for one another. That's the beautiful vision for our world given to us by the creator.

God uses the elements of trust throughout all of creation, which means we can learn from leaders beyond the church world to create, strengthen, and enhance the ways in which trust helps people work together. Therefore, this book will explore characteristics that build trust from different environments to weave together and point to the evidence of God's handiwork in building and creating trust. We will examine how these different environments use language to guide, direct, and align behaviors that help strengthen trust. Christian leaders will discover what is missing from their own faith community environments that make it difficult for people to trust the church and learn how they can work together to create places where trust can be strengthened, practiced, and enhanced. I know Christian leaders are already at work creating, designing, and adjusting systems that build trust, but the challenge we face in this time and place is doing this with intentionality, determination, humility, and grace. Stretching out our arms and metaphorically grabbing one another's hands to connect and be part of God's vision of trust in God and trust in one another is the only way we will help our communities, our institutions, and our world address the trust deficit that exists today.

Discovering the Essentials for Trust

From the beginning of life, a person's reputation is built upon simple actions and behaviors that add to their equity of trust. Much of this trust is banked in the workplace.[5] Joel Peterson, for example, in *The Ten Laws of Trust: Building the Bonds That Make a Business Great,* shows that these "laws" are critical for any working environment to succeed. If the leader puts these laws in place, trust will ultimately infuse a business.[6]

These ideas are shared by Stephen Covey, who emphasized the practices of highly effective leaders. As Covey puts it, "The best leaders recognize that trust impacts us 24/7 365 days a year."[7]

---

5. Ibid.
6. Joel Peterson, *The Ten Laws of Trust: Building the Bonds That Make a Business Great* (New York: AMACOM, 2016).
7. Stephen R. Covey, "How the Best Leaders Build Trust," *LeadershipNow:Building a Community of Leaders,* May 1, 2016, http://www.leadershipnow.com/pvcovey.html.

Onora O'Neill, a philosopher and member of the British House of Lords, through books, lectures, and other communication forms presents trust and the misconceptions that exist about trust. She takes three standard views about trust and reframes them in a new light, challenging these constructions by illustrating the careful contexts in which they might be challenged. The views she challenges are the following: "One's a claim: there has been a great decline in trust, very widely believed. The second is an aim: we should have more trust. And the third is a task: we should rebuild trust." About the aim of trust she reminds us that "intelligently placed and intelligently refused trust is the proper aim."[8] In other words, we shouldn't have blind trust.

Harvard Business Review frequently shares knowledge about marketplace trust from experts in many fields. Many TED Talks, "ideas worth sharing," feature trust and building trustworthy ecological environments in any place where people engage. I've gotten several ideas from TED presenters as they explore the concepts that challenge their own contexts in which they engage the world.

Essential characteristics, attitudes, and behaviors, which I call elements, can help managers and employees trust one another in the business, work, and even home environment. These are not new concepts, but are simple ways to consider what is necessary to build trustworthy systems that translate well into religious principles for faith communities.

In faith communities, we can't neglect our role and responsibility, because we are also affected by seismic shifts in our world, and in due course we are able to influence our world. As leaders in faith communities we should be strengthening trust in one another and in our human systems so that we are creating healthy, hope-filled communities that embody grace, peace, and love for one another. In the church realm, where there is high trust, we refer to it as the "beloved community." Beloved communities live in collaboration and connection with one

---

8. Onora O'Neill, "What We Don't Understand about Trust," *TEDxHouses of Parliament,* June 2013, https://www.ted.com/talks/onora_o_neill_what_we _don_t_understand_about_trust/transcript?language=en.

another as we do our part through interconnected systems that rely upon the actions, attitudes, and behaviors of each person. Trust is high when we feel safe, secure, and at peace within the community. When we can trust our neighbors to care about their well-being as well as our well-being, we can engage in the world with more confidence and security. There is a privilege to the beloved community that should be available to all human beings who trust each other. Unfortunately, our trust deficit restricts this privilege, and our own lack of trust limits this possibility when we become overrun by fear of neighbor and distrust of strangers. We each have a role in building and designing systems of trust that enable the beloved community to become a reality for every human being willing to participate.

The Trust Design

Now faith, hope, and love remain—these three things—and the greatest of these is love. (1 Cor 13:13)

Most of the identified actions and behaviors for fostering trust are foundational for strengthening our top three Christian moral virtues, sometimes called "spiritual gifts": faith, hope, and love. For example, by acting competently, reliably, and with integrity, you are strengthening the value of your perceived faithfulness, which in turn is essential to building trust. The business writers (Feltman, Peterson, and Covey) name competence, reliability, and integrity as characteristics needed for building trust. Onara O'Neill states that we raise three questions when we judge someone's trustworthiness: "Are they competent? Are they honest? Are they reliable? And if we find that a person is competent in the relevant matters, and reliable and honest, we'll have a pretty good reason to trust them, because they'll be trustworthy."[9] The Christian practices of faith, hope, and love point to God's expectation for trust.

In the following chapters, we'll look at these three practices and the behaviors that strengthen these practices. I'll present the problems in the

---

9. Ibid.

world and in faith communities that indicate the trust deficit caused by the weakened virtue. Then we examine the biblical evidence of change in attitudes, actions, and behaviors that strengthened this Christian moral virtue. And then I point to the twenty-first century evidence in the Western cultural context that shows where God is at work in helping in the design for systems of trust. At the end of each chapter, I invite you to examine your own behaviors, intentions, and attitudes and check your trust alignment. Are you hooked into your Christian virtues so that you can be a part of God's work through trust? How do we help others hook into those virtues so that God can use them for the beautification of this world?

High-trust cultures can do some amazing things for the sake of God's mission in the world. In a high-trust culture people operate out of a sense of faith for the community and the vision that the community is seeking to live into. In a high-trust culture there is a great deal of hope that things will be better than the current circumstance, and in a high-trust culture there is a great deal of love. On LinkedIn, a popular website for sharing your skills and abilities to succeed in the work world, a popular author and speaker, Simon Sinek, shares his quotations. One that I shared recently said, "True love exists in business. It's when employee and employer are amazingly grateful to have each other. We should all have true love at work."[10] I am drawn to this saying because in my experience of high-trust cultures, there really is a deep sense of gratitude for the people who work in those environments every day. For example, in college I was waiting tables. It was one of my early jobs after high school. I worked hard, and I wanted to make the customers more satisfied with my service. One day, the owner of the restaurant said to one of the managers, "Servers are a dime a dozen. Doesn't really matter if they come or go." Ouch. That stung because I recognized that this owner saw very little value in what I had to offer. So I quit, and I went to work for a restaurant that valued its employees and did all they could to ensure that the employees were taken care of so that the customers would be taken

10. Simon Sinek, "Start with Why," February 17, 2017, https://www.linkedin.com/in/simonsinek/.

care of in the restaurant. The servers at the second restaurant I worked at were much more satisfied. They trusted management because they knew management cared about them. Out of that high-trust culture, they created a memorable and delightful experience for the customer. This is "true love," for leader and worker. Shouldn't this kind of love be characteristic for people of faith? Christian employers and employees ought to be living these values in every place and space they live and work, so that the spiritual gifts of faith, hope, and love are visible to all.

Trust really is something that affects us all the time in every place. When there are deep fissures in trust, then creativity, innovation, and imagination are stunted by the brokenness of our human desires. But when we put our whole trust in God's faithfulness, God's hope for God's people, and God's abundant and everlasting love, we can be captured by the divine imagination and unleashed for creative, innovative wonders that make us stand in awe of the creator. That's the kind of design I hope we discover when we carefully evaluate the spiritual gifts available to us in God's creation.

Trust → Faith

Can You Seriously Trust the Church?

An article shared on Facebook lists top reasons the millennial generation lost faith in the church as an institution that is expected to model, practice, and exemplify trust in our world today. I wanted to be surprised by this lack of faith in the church and in Christians in general, but I had many experiences where I was right there with the millennials, asking the same kinds of questions about the church and wondering if this was really the place where I could "put my whole trust in God's grace." The article indicated that "59% of Millennials who were raised in the church have dropped out," and one of the main reasons highlighted by the author was, "Millennials, more than any other generation, don't trust institutions, for we have witnessed over and over how corrupt and self-serving they can be."[1] When faith in the institution is substituted for God and our reasons for why we have the body of Christ, the infrastructure for trust begins to disintegrate. Most millennials are able to see through this difference, which calls our attention to the things that need to change. The question is, do we know how to listen, and do we know how to change and adapt? Do we know how to reclaim our faith in God

---

1. Sam Eaton, "59 Percent of Millennials Raised in a Church Have Dropped Out—And They're Trying to Tell Us Why," February 9, 2017, http://faithit.com /12-reasons-millennials-over-church-sam-eaton/.

so that we can reclaim our trust in the body of Christ for the sake of God's work in the world today? Before the millennial generation grew into adults, we were already aware of lost trust in a disintegrating society. Here's what happened in the previous generation, which contributed to the dismantling of trust.

We Have No Faith in Particular!

I was born at the tail end of generation X. My generation is known for no faith in particular. Thanks to the boomer parents, this group has no faith in institutions, no faith in government, no faith in the church. For me, it felt that my generation was the pendulum swinging in the opposite direction of earlier generations in which the church experienced growth and adherence. My generation (like boomer parents before them) rebelled against the church, against institutions, and against faith in general. In fact, many in my generation left the church and are raising their children to adopt the same attitude and mentality that they have about the church. The distrust, corruption, and self-interest in the church that repulses the millennials comes from their generation X parents, if not their boomer parents as well. The church has a daunting role and responsibility in shifting these attitudes and changing these generational patterns. Leaders in the church and those who claim the Christian faith must make a conscious contribution to faith-based systems that test, enhance, and strengthen trust. How we do that will take some exploring, soul-seeking, and living our own lives as witnesses to the Christian faith so that our trust and trustworthiness points to our trust in God.

It is not surprising that generation X did not trust our institutions. The basic elements of trust are missing if not challenged since the Civil Rights era and the Vietnam War, in the experiences of the boomer generation. For the sake of this exploration, let's examine what was happening in the US cultural landscape between 1970 and 1990.

Pew Research calls generation X the "neglected 'middle child.'"[2] They noted that this generation is often absent from demographic stories and stories of change in society and politics. As the Pew researcher puts it, "They're smack in the middle innings of life, which tend to be short on drama and scant of theme."[3] They identify this generation as the bridge between major shifts and changes in the US landscape. They are not quite the boomers, nor are they like the millennials; the generation X group is the "in-between" group. Generation Xers are not completely monoracial, nor are they fully multiracial. They were growing in the number of members who claimed to be religiously unaffiliated at 21 percent of their population, whereas the millennials are at 29 percent and the boomers were at 16 percent.[4] On almost every scale shared by Pew Research, generation X members found themselves in the middle, except in the percent of gen X respondents who felt their generation to be unique. Only 49 percent felt that generation X was unique, compared to the 58 percent of boomers and the 61 percent of millennials who believe their generation is unique.[5] Maybe this is why we have accepted the term "generation X" for our generation. The "X" marking is a generic term, not unique or special. As the most current parents of children and youth, this generation of US Americans have little faith in themselves. They are the generation where faith has diminished and the pendulum has hit the bottom curve when compared to the historical generational analysis over the past thirty years.

There were major shifts in attitudes and behaviors that raised the doubt barometer in the American cultural landscape. Institutions in which trust was supposed to be the foundations of life cracked and fractured as generation X children witnessed breaking points in the system. I remember growing up with fear that the foundations of belief that I

2. Paul Taylor, "Generation X: America's Neglected 'Middle Child,'" Pew Research Center, June 15, 2014, www.pewresearch.org/fact-tank/2014/06/05/generation-x-americas-neglected-middle-child/.
3. Ibid.
4. Ibid.
5. Ibid.

was taught to trust would break the same way other foundations of trust had broken for my friends. Here's what I saw.

Marriage Is Broken

A solid family was built on the trust foundation of the institution of marriage in my young mind. In my own home, my parents seemed to have a solid and strong marriage, and that's all I knew or understood, until I saw another side of life. Kids who came from "broken homes" were typically identified as those "troubled kids," who didn't live a normal life. That was true to me until I discovered that my best friend came from a divorced home. She was being raised by a single mom and seemed to be the tough kid. But she and I got along great. She accepted me when I felt rejected by other kids because I was the lone ethnic minority kid in our predominantly white middle-class school. I didn't realize that we were both outsiders, and kids in our neighborhood were taught to not trust "outsiders." Even though my parents' marriage seemed solid, I discovered that Alley's[6] mom needed to get out of her marriage because it was abusive. It was my first experience of a crack in the institution of marriage and the first time I recognized that marriage might not be as solid and trustworthy as I thought it was for all people. Not long after my elementary school experience, I started seeing and meeting other kids whose parents were divorced or separated. With every fight my parents had, I worried that their marriage wouldn't hold up either. I lived in fear that my parents would be next. I was afraid they would fall out of love with one another and abandon their vows of mutual love and trust. If it was that easy to get out of marriage, then how could we really trust this covenant? The institution of marriage was questionable, and unfortunately the statistics were proving that in the United States marriage for life was broken. In 1980 and 1990, nearly 50 percent of all marriages ended in divorce. Today, fewer and fewer millennials are waiting to get married, if they are even willing to venture

---

6. Name changed to protect identity.

into the institution of marriage at all.[7] Therefore, the rise of doubt and distrust in marriage as a beacon for faithfulness, hopefulness, and true love were in question. Marriage as a symbol of a trustworthy relationship broke for me and many other children in my generation.

Latchkey Kids

Security in home environments also began to shift. Children who were once supervised by adults almost all the time were thrust into more and more independence as the culture changed. The rise of divorce led to an increase in single parents. In previous generations, one parent worked (usually the father) and moms stayed home. Economics, in the form of lower wages, were also beginning a shift toward two working parents, leaving children at home to raise one another. This was another marker of change from the idealistic images of families in which children could trust that a parent would always be there to supervise their activities. Latchkey kids[8] became another identifying term for this generation as families changed and life practices changed. Many had to grow up quick and learn how to take care of themselves while mom and dad were at work. They learned to trust their instincts and trust themselves.

Latchkey kids were the kids who had their house key tied to their shoe or to their backpack with a shoestring. They would jump off the bus and no one would be there to meet them. They would run home, kick off their shoes, and go straight for the fridge. Most latchkey kids

---

7. According to the Center for Disease Control's monthly report of the US Department of Health and Human Services, between 1970 and 1980 there had been a steady increase in divorces for nineteen consecutive years. Rates were still tracking about half of marriages per population of 1,000 were ending in divorce. After 1996, states stopped tracking and verifying the information. According to the CDC statistics, even though the population has increased, the rate of marriages in the United States has also significantly declined, and the number of divorces have also declined, but remain half of every marriage. (See https://www.cdc.gov/nchs/nvss/marriage-divorce.htm for more information.)

8. "Children who are regularly left without adult supervision during a significant portion of the day, referred to as 'latchkey children,' are a growing social phenomenon" ("Latchkey Children," US National Library of Medicine, accessed May 10, 2017, https://www.ncbi.nlm.nih.gov/pubmed/8987338).

would go for the best junk food they could find and then head straight for the TV. These children grew up on multiple hours of MTV or *Full House* learning how to be cool, in-fashion rockers who could navigate the world on their own. They didn't need anyone. They were completely independent, able to take care of themselves and their siblings until mom or dad got home a few hours later. And if they didn't make it home in time, they could get some food and be entertained by more sitcoms throughout the rest of the night. Latchkey kids didn't need anything but a loaf of bread, a jar of peanut butter, and a jar of strawberry or grape jelly. Their ideology was independence, and the longer they were home alone, the more they trusted themselves over anybody else.

This was the time and space where independent attitudes arose, and they realized that the most trustworthy of people would have to be "me, myself and I." Sociologists noted in 1996 that a potential consequence is the impairment of parent-child relationships. Trust in parents started fracturing, and self-reliance was a foundation that seeped into the ways in which they operated in the culture, in their homes, and even in the church (if anyone brought them to church). Whatever motivations may have been, more and more children were left at home, and trust in one's own ability to survive became the driving factor in this cultural landscape.

Abuse of Children in the Church

If you can't trust the institution of marriage and you can't trust the safety and security parents are supposed to provide, then you *should* be able to trust the church as a safe space. Unfortunately, the place where the brand is built upon an understanding of trust, safety, and security for children also fell prey to the loss of trust. Even worse was the denial of the church leadership that they had people who could not be trusted through the ministries in their church. The sacred trust fell apart.

The most notorious evidence for broken trust was portrayed in an award-winning movie. *Spotlight* (2015) dramatized the Catholic church's scandalous neglect of child-abuse cases by priests in parishes across the Boston region. So many people were choosing to look the other way because they could not face the possibility that a "person of God" could or would ever do anything to harm children. One of the most foundational institutions in the community was harboring abusers and not allowing justice to be served, or healing to begin, for the sake of maintaining the lifelong and irrevocable sanctity of the priesthood. During this time, many denominations produced new curriculum attempting to make sanctuaries safe for children and youth. They instilled two-adult policies for every Sunday school classroom and background checks on any leader working with kids. They created policies that required every church to create standard procedures to address the potential liabilities that might occur when working with children and youth. Some leaders in the church embraced these changes, while others were appalled that the church wouldn't "trust them" with the children or youth. After all, hadn't they been a member in this congregation all their lives? Why would they ever want to do anything to hurt or harm another person, let alone a child or youth? That should have been the proper response in any day and age for the people who called themselves Christian. And yet, after decades and in some cases centuries of silence about abuse, the policies were necessary because even the church was subject to human frailties and broken trust.

If you can't trust the church, then who can you trust? How on earth could anyone trust God, if the people who were supposed to be closest to Christ, living under the covenantal relationship with Christ, had broken trust? Coming back from this damaging silence seemed impossible, and in some victims' eyes may still be impossible to this day.

Broken Trust Was Justified

In each of these examples, we can see how certain behaviors diminished trust in institutions. For example, when marriages are falling apart and divorce rates are on the rise, children observe that their parents aren't really sincere about the marriage covenant. They observe that the once stable environment they lived in is no longer reliable as parents separate and the new norm includes having to go between two homes. Even in the case of abusive partners, children witness a lack of care between their parents, which also results in the broken trust of the marriage covenant. For some, marriage for both the parents and the children isn't matching the dreams they once envisioned. The elements of trust, such as sincerity, reliability, competence, and care,[9] are damaged by the perceptions and realities in these institutions.

A number of other examples over the past twenty to thirty years further justify the deep lack of trust that seems to persist in the American culture. The current political climate in the United States continues to challenge people to think about who they can trust. Can they trust the news sources? Or do they trust the political leader's words? Can we truly trust banks, or will they do something terrible with our hard-earned money? Are the products businesses sell us really trustworthy? It depends. And ultimately, many believe that God's people have failed, the leaders of institutions have failed, even our own parents have failed us. Therefore the bar of trust has been obliterated, and we operate lacking trust in anyone, any institution, and any system. We can only trust ourselves, and yet we must find ways to really trust others. Our communities cannot operate without trust. Finding ways to rebuild it through faith will be our challenge.

I point to generation X's lack of faith, because this generation is now in its most generative years, according to Erikson's psycho-social development.[10] We are raising the next generation and shaping values, beliefs, and behaviors in the next generation through our own attitudes, beliefs, and behaviors. If we are going to teach trust, we must dismantle, reteach, and rebuild trust in parents and some grandparents so what we pass on is a new understanding of trust built on the foundation of faith. We must reestablish behaviors that help build trust for future generations in our world. Our challenge will be to rebuild faith through

9. Charles Feltman, *The Thin Book of Trust: An Essential Primer for Building Trust at Work* (Bend, OR: Thin Book Publishing, 2009), Loc. 89 of 1143 E-Book.

10. Erik Erikson offered the psycho-social crisis development scale that states that people between twenty and forty-seven years of age are in middle adulthood. In middle adulthood we are either generative or stagnant. Generativity research claims that this is the most important stage in ensuring a future for the next generations. See my dissertation on spiritual generativity for more information.

consistent actions and behaviors that strengthen trust in God and trust in each other. We must also rebuild our understanding of human limitations and reimagine what trust in God means for a new generation. These are necessary steps of action if we are to change hearts and lives within our faith communities and equip trustworthy leaders who exemplify trust through their faith in God and faith in neighbor.

Biblical Elements of Trust → Faith

This isn't the first time more than one generation of people lost faith in the institutions that represent God. It isn't the first time people lost faith in the government or in businesses or in other people. Plenty of biblical examples show where faith is challenged and behaviors or lack of certain behaviors lead to broken trust. The Old Testament and the New Testament contain numerous stories about trust between God and the people, and even more stories showing the loss of trust in God or each other because of human failures.

So, why trust again? We ask ourselves this question when we experience one broken trust after another. I find myself thinking, *I can't trust anyone.* But that doesn't seem like the right answer, so I wonder what trust means as a faithful person who attempts to put trust in God.

If I can't trust Christians, then can I really trust God? Is it possible to trust God and not trust my neighbors? If I must trust again because of my faith, then how do I get past my suspicions and skepticism of my neighbors? Are faith and trust synonymous? Is it possible to have faith and not trust God? Is it possible to trust God and not have faith? What do we mean when we trust the faithfulness of Jesus? Can we really call ourselves people of faith if we don't trust our Christian leaders?

It would be a relief if there were simple answers, but building trust through our faith can be a challenging theological task.

Before we dig into the theological exploration of trust, let's establish a definition of faith. Because of my faith in God, I have faith in people who claim to practice the Christian faith. I observe that they have a set of beliefs and values that guide their actions and behaviors, which are similar to my beliefs and values. I trust them and am interested and willing to build a relationship with them based upon that trust grounded in those beliefs and values. Therefore, I have confidence that they respect humanity and seek to do no harm to humanity. I have confidence that people who practice the Christian faith are striving to do what's right in the most general terms and experiences. I was taught this through my parents' actions of faith that led them to trust.

An interesting observation of this approach appears in the way we talk about Jesus. Our emphasis has been on believing in Jesus, which is well documented in the Bible as our primary invitation to trust. However, belief is a cognitive emphasis rather than a relational emphasis. The cognitive emphasis makes us focus on the rationality of the story and the experience. This emphasis may be part of the challenge we face as we seek to understand trust in Jesus. Trust is the relational emphasis that is strengthened by the action of faith. Here's an example of trust through faith.

When I was twelve years old, I was elected to serve on a national board for my denomination that would require me to travel to another city in another state. At that time, the board paid for members to travel to those meetings, but didn't really pay for other family members to attend. My dad was a pastor and my mom a nursing assistant, and we didn't have a lot of extra income to travel. So my parents had faith that the people from this board would take care of me because they were leaders in the church. Because of this faith in leadership and this faith in the church, they trusted me to go to Washington, DC by myself and navigate the travel to get to this board meeting on my own. Their faith in the Christian institution and the leaders of that institution led them to trust their eldest child to this faith community hundreds of miles away. Of course, the world seemed safer then, but there was nothing in their experience in the culture that told them not to have faith in the institution or the leadership of the institution. It appeared to be a high-trust culture, and trust was reinforced when I was welcomed into the community, cared for by the leaders in that community, and then returned safely to my family. Their faith in the Christian leaders of this institution led them to trust, and the leader's actions reinforced that act of trust. With this understanding of faith as trust, let's see if biblical stories and theological interpretation will illustrate how faith can lead to trust, and why trust can be reinforced by our faith.

Old Testament: Learning to Trust through Faith in God

In the first story of creation, we discover an invitation to believe and trust that creation is good. "God saw everything he had made: it was supremely good" (Gen 1:31).

What makes us trust the created order of God's world and have faith that it is good? We trust through our own experience of creation and the creative process. We watch the sunrise, and we see that it is good. We see the mountains, and we stand in awe and wonder. We come to the ocean, and we experience a vastness that is beyond our imagination. We trust these words because we witness and experience the faithfulness of the sun rising each day and giving us light. We trust the creation story because we see the evidence of creation in our everyday lives. As creators and as creation, we trust that life exists by the power of something beyond ourselves and our own understanding. Perhaps this is why we are able to open our imaginations in Genesis 1, suspend our skepticism, and have faith that our creator desires good for creation. It is the first step, the first invitation to trust through faith in God.

Other stories in the Old Testament bear witness to ancestors who had faith in God, in humanity, and in themselves. They also bear witness to the consequences of putting trust in human endeavor rather than divine endeavor. Noah, for example, put his faith completely in God as he responded to God's call, God's plan, and then God's wisdom to take care of Noah and his descendants. It was the first step of faith that helped Noah put his full trust in God as he ventured into an unknown future.

21

Genesis 6:13 describes Noah's response to God's invitation. God sees humanity fail and make mistakes in many ways, which means God no longer trusts humanity to respect creation. But God trusts Noah who is faithful. Noah is sincere in how he has taken care of God's creation and his own family. Noah demonstrates reliability and competence as he begins to build a very large boat to hold God's creation. God also provides Noah with clear directions, a clear vision, and belief in Noah's ability to respond. Trust is built between God and between Noah with each small step in the story. We discover this interchange of God's faith in Noah to be trustworthy and responsive. We see Noah's faith in God as he follows the directions and then experiences the vision. As the rains fall and the ark holds steadfast, Noah's faith increases and he invites his family to have faith in the vision God sets before them. Noah's faith increases as each day passes, and the food is sufficient for the animals and his family. Noah's faith is tested when the days grow long and the waters don't subside. And yet he trusts that God will deliver what God promises because God is faithful in everything thus far. God is consistent and God is faithful.

In hindsight, it is easy to see God's faithfulness, but when living in the moment and the days seem to go on and on, there probably were moments when Noah wondered, and perhaps his faith even wavered as he waited for God to respond by clearing the waters. But the story tells us that God carried out God's promise, and Noah and his descendants were blessed because they trusted God and God trusted them.

Abraham's story is a foundational covenant that God made between God and the people. We are introduced to Abraham in Genesis 11:27 when he is named as one of three sons born to Terah. His given name was Abram at birth and he marries Sarai. After the death of Abram's father, God invites Abram into a deeper relationship by promising blessings and faithfulness to Abram.

The LORD said to Abram, "Leave your land, your family, and your father's household for the land that I will show you. I will make of you a great nation and will bless you. I will make your name respected, and you will be a blessing. I will bless those who bless you, those who curse you I will curse; all the families of the earth will be blessed because of you." (Gen 12:1-3)

Abraham exercised much faith in his relationship with God as he entered into a new covenant that strengthened and tested Abraham's commitment to this relationship and God's ability to keep the promises made to Abraham. Four significant moments test Abraham's faith and obedience to God. The first moment was noted in Genesis 12 in the invitation to leave his homeland, his country, and all that was familiar and secure for him to follow where God was leading. The second moment was identified as the time when he and his nephew Lot parted company in order to keep the peace amongst their households (Gen 13:1-16). The third event familiar to most Christians was the promise that Abraham would have descendants and be "the ancestor of many nations" (Gen 17:4). This moment was hard to believe because Abraham was already ninety-nine years old and Sarah was also too old to bear children. But God made a promise, and out of that promise and his delight in Abraham's obedience, Abraham and Sarah brought Isaac into the world as a gift from God. This occasion reveals how faithful God is to the covenant and how reliable God is in Abraham's life. God's trust in Abraham was undeniable.

Abraham's trust in God was also beyond our limited imagination. The last moment noted about Abraham's faithfulness to God was the moment he took his only son, Isaac, to the mountain to offer him as a sacrifice to God, obedient to God's command (Gen 22). He did not question, wonder, or argue with God about the rationale for this seemingly insane request; he completely put his trust in God and set out to follow through on this directive. God, with infinite wisdom, responded faithfully to Abraham's action and provided him with the ram that would take his son's place. This is a kind of faith that seems hard for us to wrap our minds around in a twenty-first-century mission context, but this story is the foundation for our understanding of the character of God and God's trustworthiness. Not only is Abraham the father of the Christian faith, but so many other world religions find a connection with the Abrahamic story. He is the epitome of trust built through faith in God and God's faith in God's creation.

Another foundational relationship from the Old Testament comes in Exodus. In Exodus, we meet Moses's parents from the Levite tribe, and we discover what faith looks like from many points of view. His life was filled with faithful people putting their trust in God rather than in the customs and laws of Egypt. It started with two midwives whose faith in God helped them save Hebrew babies from certain death. This trust in God led them to take actions that put their lives at risk. Next, Moses's biological mother put her trust in God as she risked saving Moses's life. Moses's big sister learned about this faith in God through her mother's actions and her mother's command to watch her brother. Her trust in God's faithfulness and wisdom was confirmed when she saw Pharaoh's daughter come to the water to find the baby floating in a reed boat. She risked being exposed as she carefully approached Pharaoh's daughter to offer her mother as the nurse who could care for this child. With each action, their trust in God's faithfulness was deepened, enhanced, and strengthened as Moses grew up to be a faithful leader who put his whole trust in God.

Many other story collections in the Old Testament (Joseph, Deborah, David, Ruth) give witness to God's faithfulness. These narratives confirm that God's blessings follow from our trust in God's faithfulness because we witness the good that God does through us as partners with God's creation. If we have faith we will discover God's trust in us and thereby learn to trust God.

New Testament: A Baby Is Sent to Reset Faith

We've had trust issues from the beginning of time, and it seems to be a cyclical problem when you read the stories about Israel from Deuteronomy through 2 Kings. Our history with God shows us that faith, hope, and love lead to trust, with the consequence that broken trust diminishes faith, hope, and love. While the cycles are shown to us through stories over many centuries in the Old Testament, the New Testament hits a reset button for the future. Jesus comes at a time when God seems to be losing faith again in the human race and its institutions, such as the Roman Empire. God sees that trust is at the bottom. People don't trust God, and God struggles with the creation. What must God do to rebuild trust and show us that God has faith in us? God enters the world in the most innocent, trusting form known to humankind (see Matt 1:18-24; Luke 1:26–2:38).

A baby is the most trusting creation of the human form. A baby can do nothing on his or her own, except learn to trust that another human will take care of his or her every need. A baby comes into the world helpless, and therefore must completely rely on the intuition of the parent to do good for him or her. The New Testament tells us that God chose to come into the world in this form, the form of a baby. Why? Because God risked that parents would do the right thing and take care of God in this infant form, innocent and completely reliant upon the world. Jesus is God's next step in resetting faith when the world is working against the values of trust through faith. God shows the world that humanity can be reliable, and so God chose a young woman and a young man to carry forth the story of creation. The incarnation is how God places divine faith in a human creation.

The Christmas story is God's restoration of faith in humanity, so that we can once again have faith in God and trust God's abundant love and unmerited grace. The New Testament stories during Advent each year are God's invitations to reset faith and trust. Through our annual rituals as we wait for Christ's coming, we are connected to God and to each other. Anyone can relate to the story of a baby, and we all remember how as infants we had no choice but to trust the people who brought us into this world. As infants in a modern world we trust doctors, nurses, and "institutions" that employ educated, equipped people to take care of us. As a parent, we trust historical actions and experiences of others as they bring infants into the world. Whether through the wisdom of midwifery or the professionalism of hospitals, we trust these institutions. God wisely chose and chooses an incarnation to help us reset faith so that we might be able to trust God over and over again, even when the world fails us.

As we reconstruct our own understanding of trust so that the future of our Christian witness is changed, we can begin to see how a baby is the perfect illustration of trust. That is the first gift of the New Testament. A baby has always signaled and continues to signal to the possibilities of new life. A baby shows us that things can be different and joining the creator in shaping a life for this child invites us to be more trustworthy as we embrace the sacred trust of parenting. Thus God's faith in us to care for new life strengthens our faith in God, the giver of all life.

Cultural Designs for Trust → Faith

Stephen Covey, well-known author of *The 7 Habits of Highly Effective People*, reminds us that trust is necessary 24 hours a day, 7 days a week, 365 days a year.[11] In my faith community we talk about our discipleship mission as dependent on a "web of interactive relationships"[12] throughout the world. In every community around the world, an ebb and flow of relationships with families, friends, and even complete strangers affects how we interact in this world. Our actions, reactions, behaviors, and attitudes can strengthen, enhance, and illuminate trust or it can destroy and eliminate trust. The systems we create and contribute to are often built because of our faith. For example, in church systems, it is our faith in God that invites us to develop systems that contribute to human flourishing. We believe in God's goodness, and therefore we want what is good for ourselves, our families, and for others. Therefore, our trust in God's goodness, God's desire for the whole creation, and God's grace through the son, Jesus, leads us to faith in God

11. Stephen M. R. Covey, "How the Best Leaders Build Trust," accessed June 9, 2017, https://leadershipnow.com/CoveyOnTrust.html.

12. *Book of Discipline of The United Methodist Church,* paragraph 125.

and faith in the people whom God creates. Therefore, as God's creation, we are each invited to have faith in one another, which helps us learn to trust one another. My story illustrates how my parents' faith in God led them to have confidence in God's leaders, which in turn allowed them to trust their child to travel across the country alone.

This interaction between our beliefs, our confidence, and our willingness to trust leads to our creation of systems reliant upon this *web of interactive relationships.* In my Christian tradition, the Methodists recognized these necessary interactions, which established a trust that they teach, preach, and exemplify. The Methodist movement in the United States planted the seeds of education, physical health, and spiritual renewal throughout the country and beyond. Many schools, hospitals, and faith-based institutions were founded after the Civil War and through the first half of the twentieth century, based on the Methodist desire for human flourishing. These institutions continue to be critical in the American landscape, because they provide a foundation for trust.

We now explore how our faith in these different systems helps our faith and hope throughout the world. Through these examples we can see the beauty of well-designed trust as we seek to restore the vision of trust God has in mind for faithful people.

Faith in Health Systems

If God entered the world as a helpless trusting infant, notice that in nearly every society in the world the health systems are also dependent on the faithfulness and trust of the designers. We believe that doctors and nurses are trained to help people get better and become or stay healthy. Every person privileged enough to read this book has been to a doctor and has faith that what the doctor does and can do is heal you and help you. Through this faith, we trust that what an expert is telling us is true because they have studied the subject or seen the problem before, have learned from others and practiced competently enough to pass exams designed by other expert doctors. And people studying to be doctors trust that those expert doctors have enough experience to know what works and doesn't work, and they care enough to pass that information along. By using characteristics of trust, we have faith that doctors as a whole are primarily reliable, have proven competence, and demonstrate sincerity and care in their field as a whole. There have been enough doctors around the world who have operated in trustworthy ways that we collectively have faith that the health industry is working for the good of humanity.

Let's look at some evidence for this faith through data, tradition, reason, and experience:[13]

Tradition

An indicator of our trust in the health system could be the number of people who are uninsured. If insurance is needed to afford and obtain decent health care, then there is some evidence that people trust health care to care for their health needs. And being insured allows you to have access to health care to meet those needs. Therefore, the number of people insured could be used as an indicator of faith in our health-care systems. The Centers for Disease Control and Prevention reported that in 2015 the percentage of people in the United States who were uninsured was at an all-time low. Only 9.1 percent (at the time of the interview) of the sample were uninsured, down by nearly 2.5 percentage points than the previous year. This is also down nearly 7 percentage points from 2010, indicating that more people are able to use the health-care systems with confidence because they are insured.[14] This can be an indicator of faith in the system, but this doesn't tell the whole story.

---

13. Albert Outler, the noted sholar of Wesleyan thought, described a quadrilateral pattern in John Wesley's approach to biblical authority: scripture, tradition, reason, and experience. In the following examples of trust and faith that characterize our confidence in relational human systems, I am adapting this four-part pattern to include "data," especially where scripture is not the driver for describing human trust in a system.

14. Robin A. Cohen, Michael E. Martinez, and Emily P. Zammitti, "Health Insurance Coverage: Early Release of Estimates from the National Health Interview Survey, 2015," accessed June 9, 2017, https://www.cdc.gov/nchs/data/nhis/early release/insur201605.pdf.

Data

Data can also help us see patterns in the traditions. Just like the stories in the scripture that point to patterns of behavior between God and humanity, data shows us patterns of behavior that illustrate changes in traditions. Trust in types of health-care providers has changed over time and even across traditions. Using the childbirth example, we can see that during the twentieth century, childbirth moved from outside of the hospital in the early 1900s to nearly always in a hospital in 1969.[15] The tradition changed because people trusted the data that was showing them babies had a greater chance of survival in hospital settings. Data was shared through the communication of lived experiences.

Experience/Reason

Deloitte Center for Health Solutions wrote an article in 2013 making the case for using health data to magnify real-world evidence of what is working to address diseases:

> Transparency and communication of the benefits of real world evidence is essential but insufficient alone to reassure sceptics. In order to build further trust across all stakeholder groups, including patients, payers, providers, clinicians, academics, regulators and the pharmaceutical industry, a mutually accepted process with governance is required for the use of health data to generate real world evidence.[16]

We see a claim about how the health industry builds trust. First of all, they communicate care. They know that people have a stake in health care and thereby tell us directly that they care about what people think and know about their health. They list the stakeholders, which nearly includes every person and even people who hold multiple

---

15. Ibid.

16. "Good Evidence Practice: Building Stakeholder Trust in Use of Health Data," Deloitte Centre for Health Solutions, accessed May 10, 2017, https://www2 .deloitte.com/content/dam/Deloitte/uk/Documents/life-sciences-health-care /deloitte-uk-good-evidence-practice.pdf.

roles. Providers, academics, and regulators are also patients and payers. They show us what competence looks like by appealing to consensus regulations that are designed through governance. They state that it is a "mutually accepted process," again appealing to the reader that they are trustworthy because they understand what is and isn't accepted in the field. This example gives evidence and data that makes the claim, "If many people experience this and we chronicle their experiences, then the evidence tells us it must be a true and trustworthy experience that can be replicated." This is one of the ways we come to have faith in our doctors and nurses as they are designed today.

Faith in Education Systems

In the United States, we have faith in our education systems, though like health care that faith is always under stress. Nearly every parent sends their child to some form of general education, with exception for those few who do it themselves at home. The education systems are designed to reinforce our faith in the betterment of humanity and human productivity. We believe that by educating our children, we are making them become better people, able to contribute to the world, and able to contribute to their own sustainable being. Therefore, we place our faith in educational systems that have been the most traditional ways of preparing our children to participate in our communities and our world. Even though public and private schools may have some differences, a majority of school systems operate with teachers and students in varied learning environments. We regularly place our trust in the expertise of teachers to train, equip, and empower our children to grow into our cultural expectations and norms. Therefore, by choice, we indicate that we have faith in our school systems. Of course, there are outliers and failures and alternative education models, but according to traditions, data, experience, and reason, we put our faith in school systems and thereby trust that the outcomes of better children for the world is accomplished through these systems.

Tradition

Traditionally my family sends our children to the public schools. My ancestors, who were born and raised in the Philippines, sent their children to the local public school because they had faith that the school would teach them to be better people and better citizens. For my parents nearly fifty years ago, that confidence was a sacrifice, because the children could have been used on their farm or in their homes. But my grandparents on both sides of the family sent them to the public school with a teacher in a classroom filled with students of the same age. Therefore, they sent me to public school, and I send my children to the public school today. For the average US family, this is the practice and the tradition.

Data

The data tells the same story. By looking at indicators of confidence in a primary school's ability to prepare young people to be contributors to society and the world, we hone in on high school graduation rates. I assume that students who participate in the twelve-year grade level system have faith that a high school diploma has value for their life. Therefore, high school graduation rates are an indicator that achieving the high school diploma became a higher priority for students than other potentially distracting factors, like working for pay, pregnancies, alcohol, drugs, and so forth. Because educators and other community leaders have faith that high school graduation matters for the betterment of the community, these leaders rallied together to help ensure that students have every opportunity to complete their education.

According to the National Center for Education Statistics, between 1910 and 2015, the high school graduation rate increased by 75 percent.[17] This means that over the last century we have increased our faith in the primary education systems in the United States. Trust for these systems has increased, and the data has also shown that schools have

---

17. "Digest of Education Statistics," National Center for Education Statistics, accessed May 10, 2017, https://nces.ed.gov/programs/digest/d15/tables/dt15_104.10.asp?current=yes.

improved the quality of life for students and for the communities in which they engage.

There are countless articles that speak of the value of education for societies. For example, everyone knows that completing a high school education opens the doors for more work opportunities and, statistically speaking, those with a bachelor's degree earn 62 percent more than those with only a high school diploma.[18] We trust the data because the data reflects our experience.

Experience/Reason

People tend to say "trust your experience" when they are talking about decision making in our world. Most people do trust their experience as they engage in systems designed for trust. Educational systems reinforce confidence by producing critical thinkers, better researchers, and more thoughtful problem solvers. Therefore, educational systems earn the faith of the people because people experience the benefits of education, through income and through work opportunities. Therefore, it is reasonable to say that we put our faith in education systems and we trust that they will equip our children to be better members of society.

Another reason the education systems are designed for trust is that they have agreements called "industry standards," which convince the employers that graduates have the basic knowledge, skills, and abilities to do the job they are entering. Employers trust certain educational institutions to prepare their people to do the job to a standard that allows them to excel in the field they are working. The more an educational institution provides students who are better prepared, have more experience, and perform in the industry with excellence, the more people in the industry trust the education. It's a system designed to build, sustain, and strengthen trust when all participants operate faithfully within the system.

18. "What Is the Value of Education in the U.S.?" Learn.org, accessed May 10, 2017, http://learn.org/articles/What_is_the_Value_of_Education_in_the_US.html.

By using the four-part evidence structure for discerning the trust that makes a human system effective, you can begin to see how interlocked and intertwined systems are in order for trust to exist, grow, and strengthen. In these systems, we trust the data that is shared when other "trustworthy" people are the ones sharing the data. We trust the traditions when other people we trust share their experience with those particular traditions. We trust our experiences when it is confirmed by other trustworthy people's experiences as well. At some point we take the "leap of faith" when we commit to have faith that this system is worthy of our trust.

Trust → Leap of Faith

We take a "leap of faith" (Søren Kierkegaard's phrase[19]) to strengthen and build trust. Just as Abraham took a "leap of faith" in Genesis 22, God risked creating humanity as a leap of faith. God has the ability and power to create something supremely good. God took another leap of faith through creation by coming into the world as an infant, completely and wholly dependent on human parents in order to live and survive. The first time we walk into a hospital or send our children into a school, we are taking a leap of faith into systems that are designed for trust. The leap of faith is about believing in these hospitals, schools, and communities and thereby putting our trust in the system and choosing to be a trustworthy participant in that system.

In our daily existence we operate on systems of trust, and for the most part, despite the potential for great harm and self-destruction, humanity eventually proves itself trustworthy. The world has increased in population, and most places in the world are sustained by systems of trust through community organization, governmental disciplines, and belief systems that are foundational to reinforcing systems of trust. If you look around, you'll begin to see how faith is an effective anchor

---

19. Søren Kierkegaard, "Fear and Trembling," *Cambridge University Press,* accessed June 9, 2017, http://assets.cambridge.org/97805218/48107/front matter/9780521848107_frontmatter.pdf.

for the beautiful creation of trust. God as creator took a leap of faith in creating humanity. As we explore this design, we begin to see signs of the evidence that God has faith in God's creation and because of that faith, we too can be a part of the beautiful design of trust.

Questions to Consider

Biblical Stories

1. What other stories in the Bible illustrate how God put God's faith in humanity as a first step of trust?

2. What stories in the Bible illustrate how humanity put faith in God and where God responded to strengthening trust by being reliable?

Cultural Systems

1. What other cultural systems exist in our societies that are dependent on the first leap of faith for them to operate (e.g., consider someone who tried a product or used the product first before trusting the product or the producer's competency)?

2. What are some of the elements that need to be in place for people to take that leap of faith?

3. What do you believe needs to be in place for you to take a leap of faith in a new product or a new company?

Trust → Hope

We have access by faith into this grace in which we stand through him, and we boast in the hope of God's glory. But not only that! We even take pride in our problems, because we know that trouble produces endurance, endurance produces character, and character produces hope. This hope doesn't put us to shame, because the love of God has been poured out in our hearts through the Holy Spirit, who has been given to us. (Rom 5:2-5)

I've often wondered what it means to have character that produces hope. But as I reflect on this scripture and think about ways in which I examine trust, I have come to an understanding that hope and trust are intertwined. Trust is used to describe hope, and hope is a sense that is lived out through actions that convey trust. Hope is about a feeling of anticipation and expectation, according to formal dictionary definitions.[1] It inspires us to act in a variety of ways. Hope is a fundamental Christian value that is brought to life through our scriptural witness, our tradition, our experiences, and our reason. I am one who acts on hope, which sometimes leads me to actions that illustrate my trust. Hope is what keeps me moving forward in life in so many ways. I have hope that my church will find a better way to live together in the midst of our diversities, and therefore I trust that my actions will help find that way. I have hope that the leadership in countries around the world will see the challenges, hear the voices of those who are oppressed and

---

1. Google search, accessed May 10, 2017, https://www.google.com/search?q=hope&rlz=1C5CHFA_enUS722US722&oq=hope&aqs=chrome..69i57j0l5.690j0j4&sourceid=chrome&ie=UTF-8.

impoverished, and make better decisions for all, and therefore I trust that my contributions in this world may help those leaders see those challenges and hear those voices. I have hope that God's wisdom will prevail, and people will experience the love, joy, peace, and possibility that life has to offer when we live into a vision of trust in God and trust in our neighbors. Because I hope, I am willing to take the leap of faith to trust. Trust is and can be strengthened because we have the gift of hope in the good of people and the good of God's creation and through the hope we can see the possibilities of trustworthy relationships with one another. Hope grounded in Jesus Christ is different than naïve optimism. With a vision of hope through Christ, we can trust that God can do good in the midst of our adversities, while acknowledging that our optimism may not always change the outcomes of the disparate circumstances that exist in our world. But, because of our hope through Christ, we can take action and communicate why we trust God and why we are willing to trust one another in our world. We can build foundations of trust, and we can invite people to trust each other, because we have hope that God can and does create good out of our faithful responses. Without some sense of hope we find it difficult to trust. But is it possible to have trust without hope? Is it possible to hope without some sense of trust? Can they be separated from each other?

Why Hope Seems in Danger of Being Lost

I tend to be an optimistic person who believes the best in people. But through my experiences over the past few years in various leadership positions in the church I serve, it makes me wonder if I still have the gift of hope, and if because of that lack of hope, it's making me reticent to trust. I have witnessed and listened to leaders in the church, as they point blame at the people who represent extreme positions on the issues of same-sex marriage and ordination. Some of these leaders blame one side or the other for the decline and demise of the denomination.[2] The suspicion is so intense that a bishop presiding over a denominational meeting can be accused of sending hand signals to delegates on how they should vote. Church leaders often come out of controversial meetings more angered, distraught, and discouraged by the words, actions, and behaviors of good Christian people who have deeply rooted differences. In my church denominaton, I find it difficult to see the evidence for the binding, energizing gift of hope. The voices that prevail in my sources of information believe we are on the brink of a division that can't be undone. Divisions across the churches and denominations can destroy our ability to give hope to one another, to bequeath hope to our institutions, and to have much hope for a better, peaceful world.

Hope certainly seems to be in short supply when we hear the news each day. In Orlando, Florida, at the Pulse nightclub, fifty people were shot dead and at least fifty-three were wounded. Motivated by hate, the gunman walked in and opened fire on innocent, unknowing people he thought were lesbian, gay, bisexual, or transgender. As the war in Syria escalated to an unfathomable genocide on the Syrian countryside, refugees caught in the crossfire of an unforgiving civil war risked their lives to flee to cities such as Aleppo. It certainly seems as though there are more stories of hopelessness than there are stories of trust in the world in recent years. It's hard to focus on the stories of hope when we scan the broader landscape and the protruding more visible stories are those that illustrate the despair that seems prevalent.

A good friend from Syria lost hope for her home country. She observes how people on the ground in her country don't trust the people who say they want to help. She showed me pictures of people whom she trusted, who kept telling her that what is reported through the news and on social media isn't true. The ceasefire wasn't honored when humanitarian buses sent to rescue refugees were set on fire. She describes the heartbreaking story of a bus driver, there to do his job, who was killed because the buses were targeted and destroyed. There is no hope when warring

---

2. Readers interested in exploring this claim can find multiple blogs that illustrate extreme positions across the Christian churches and in theological schools.

groups can't be trusted to care about the innocent bystanders who want to live and be safe. For her all hope is lost.

As I witness the divisions among public leaders, religious communities, and political factions, I wonder if anybody is willing to cross these lines and find ways to work together for a better future for all. When we stay isolated in our opinions and ideals, we magnify the distrust that grows when there are divisions. And as distrust grows, we can easily find ourselves spiraling into hopelessness. There are too many places in this world where hope seems lost and the culture of trust is extremely low.

With technology expanding, we have so much access to story after story that seems desperate, discouraging, and downright depressing. I scan Facebook and Twitter and get access to tragedies happening all over the world. The news is constantly bombarding us with killings, mass murders, gang violence, oppression, unstable countries and communities because people disregard one another's humanity and their right to flourish. Police versus black men, conservatives versus liberals, hate groups versus people of color, rich versus poor, immigrants versus native-born, educated versus those with only limited exposure to education—you name it, if there is a difference, people will find it and use it to escalate hatred, anger, and fear of the "other." Where is hope? Should we even have hope? Or do we find ourselves living more as people in despair? As people in despair, how can we even learn to trust each other in a hopeless world? When I am overcome with despair, these are the questions I cry out to God.

Exploring Hopelessness

It's hard to believe that we could or should act with trust through hope if we don't know how and where we have lost hope as faithful people. I'd like to explore hopelessness and what has caused it scientifically and spiritually so that we might find a way to connect our actions of trust based upon our experience of hope. By "hope," I mean the sense that people believe it possible that something good can happen, even in the midst of challenges and tragedy. John Wesley writes in his commentary on Romans 5 that he believes the author of the epistle is making the case that all who believe are brought into such a state of happiness and contentment through Christ that even afflictions can be turned into a matter of joy.[3] Therefore, endurance producing character is the sequence in which the development of character then produces hope, according to Romans 5:4. This kind of hope comes through our belief, our faith, and our understanding in Jesus as risen Christ who overcomes death, adversity, and even despair, and redeems all through the power of the resurrection. This hope gives us the gift to persevere even when all tangible evidence surrounding us tells us there is no hope. It is trusting that even in loss, in despair God can use our faithfulness, our circumstances, and our very lives to change the world. Jurgen Moltmann describes this as "active hope," in which he describes the nature of God being the "God of hope," and out of this hope, we can act, trusting God's promises for our future. This is "active hope" that leads us to trust in God.

The God spoken of here is no intraworldly or extraworldly God, but the "God of hope" (Rom 15:13), a God with "future as his essential nature" (as E. Bloch puts it), as made known in Exodus and in Israelite prophecy, the God whom we therefore cannot really have in us or over us but always only before us, who encounters us in his promises for the future, and whom we therefore cannot "have" either, but can only await in active hope.[4]

Hope is a gift given by the creator that we have the responsibility to steward, use, and share. Through our biblical stories, we discover where good people lost hope and what it took for them to gain it again. Through our life experiences, we see patterns of actions that were taken because of hope. Through data, we see other people who have had hope and experienced good because of that hope. Therefore we begin to believe and hope that things can and will be different from where we are currently situated in the world today. "May the God and Father of our Lord Jesus Christ be blessed! On account of his vast mercy, he has given

---

3. John Wesley, "Notes on St. Paul's Epistle to the Romans," Bible Study Tools, accessed April 13, 2017, http://www.biblestudytools.com/commentaries/wesleys-explanatory-notes/introductions/ro-intro.html.

4. Jurgen Moltmann, "Theology of Hope," *Online Journal of Public Theology,* accessed April 13, 2017, http://www.pubtheo.com/theologians/moltmann/theology-of-hope-0b.htm.

us new birth. You have been born anew into a living hope through the resurrection of Jesus Christ from the dead. You have a pure and enduring inheritance that cannot perish—an inheritance that is presently kept safe in heaven for you" (1 Pet 1:3-4). Out of this hope, we live into the future, trusting God and taking active steps in trusting our neighbor. This hope inspires in us a willingness to extend hope through trust of one another. It is a careful and sometimes risky construction when we consider human error and sin. There is a desire to not extend trust and lose hope in humanity when we are overwhelmed by despair. On the other extreme, blind optimism does not foster hope that leads to trust, either. Therefore, finding the balance that helps Christians take actions toward trust through hope can be difficult but not impossible.

A colleague from my PhD program, Meredith Hoxie Schol, gave this reflection about the difference between optimism and hope to a group of students after she attended the Paulo Freire Cátedra:

Optimism...

We often think about optimism as a belief that things will go well because...well, things *must* go well. I think there is a time and a place for optimism.

Hope...

Hope is something different (compared to optimism). It is not simply a belief about the future; it is an orientation to our current reality. When we say we have hope in Christ, it is a statement about our agency in the present.

Freire talks about the incompleteness of our humanity drawing us toward this need for hope, which manifests in our acting to change the conditions of the world...not just to become, but to "be more." Our actions illustrate our trust through hope.

Hope is one of the foundation hooks to consider when we envision the Gabriel Dawes image I shared earlier, as an illustration of the carefully crafted trust design. It is not naïve optimism, but rather an understanding of God's love, life, and promise that allows us to hold on to a spiritual vision of life that keeps us from complete despair and prompts us to take action.

The opposite of hope is despair. But when I describe hopelessness, I'm talking about the loss of passion or belief that anything will ever change and that anything could actually be different. People who are hopeless have given up—on life, on institutions, and on anything that might be perceived to produce good. In the illustrations I named earlier, hopelessness comes when the evidence for fear, doubt, and despair are greater than the passion of hope.

Some of my favorite lessons for life come through Disney movies. A Disney movie based upon a futuristic themepark offers a great example of how a glimmer of hope can shift the future. *Tomorrowland*[5] came out in 2015, and told the story of a young girl who is recruited to save the world from a predicted, ultimate demise. David Nix, played by Hugh Laurie, is the governor of Tomorrowland who uses the device created by Frank Walker, the scientist, to foresee the future of humanity. What he sees is disturbing and he believes that humanity will ultimately destroy itself. He believes that there is absolutely no hope for humanity in the future. He sees a future in which ultimate self-centered pursuit of knowledge and success overwhelms desire to do good in the world. Therefore, he rationalizes that the current world needs to be destroyed and humanity needs to be put out of their misery. He only trusted himself and the community he created and therefore believed that there can only be a better future if it were all under his control. Young Casey Newton shows David Nix and the rest of the world that even an ounce of hope can change the outcome for the future. The world will be better when more people have hope and trust each other to bring that hope into a clear vision of a better future.

When leaders prefer to walk away from one another instead of work through problems together, they come to believe there is no hope in changing each other's minds about matters they deem most important.

---

5. *Tomorrowland*, 2015 production by Walt Disney Pictures, directed by Brad Bird, http://movies.disney.com/tomorrowland.

In my denomination's history, division occurred around the matter of slavery in which the North and the South had no hope that they could convince their opponents to change their stances. Out of that posture of hopelessness, they left one another. Several years later, that hopelessness was turned back into hope when the culture changed and the leaders changed. Hope that had been lost was eventually restored.

The US popular culture through movies and music is filled with examples of hope lost and hope gained. Look at songs that try to communicate the good in humanity and the hope we should have in humanity: John Lennon's "Imagine" or Michael Jackson's "We Are the World"—or "One Tribe" by the Black Eyed Peas, whose lyrics capture the hope that we have in the goodness and possibility of humanity to see what unites them:

> One tribe, one time, one planet, one race;
> It's all one blood, don't care about your face.[6]

I believe that people want to hope in the possibility of where they can go, they want to see what will take them there, and they want to know they can achieve it. Not all hope is lost. Moltmann strengthens this resolve by stating,

> It is only in following the Christ who was raised from suffering, from a god-forsaken death and from the grave that it gains an open prospect in which there is nothing more to oppress us, a view of the realm of freedom and of joy. Where the bounds that mark the end of all human hopes are broken through in the raising of the crucified one, there faith can and must expand into hope. There its hope becomes a "passion for what is possible" (Kierkegaard), because it can be a passion for what has been made possible.[7]

---

6. "One Tribe," *The E.N.D (Energy Never Dies),* Black Eyed Peas, written by Allan Pineda, Jaime Gomez, Printz Board, Stacy Ferguson, Will Adams; copyright BMG Rights Management US, LLC, 2009.

7. Moltmann, "Theology of Hope."

Hope in the Bible

The word *hope* appears 226 times in the Common English Bible translation. From the Old Testament to the New Testament many stories illustrate how God answers with hope. We marvel at what God does through people, even when it seems as though there should be no reason to hope for a better future. As we discover how hope is intertwined in the Bible with trust, we ponder whether God needs us to hope in order for us to trust God. Why is hope necessary for the future of humanity? Why do people hold on to hope? What does the promise of the resurrection have to do with creating hope for all of God's people? Is the resurrection necessary for hope? Can we trust each other without hope?

Hopelessness Transformed into Hope: The Story of Ruth

Ruth's story shows how a person can go from utter hopelessness to a little bit of hope for a future to full trust in God. Most Christians are familiar with the story of Ruth and Naomi, but here is a short summary.

Naomi loses her husband and her sons in a very short period of time. She is widowed with two young daughters-in-law who have no children. In that time and place, having no man in your life and no sons in your life means you have no inherited property and no identity. You are invisible. So Naomi knows she can no longer have sons and has no way of helping her daughters establish value in society again. She tells them to go back to their fathers where they might be able to get married again and still have children. Her words in Ruth 1:8-17 convey the hopelessness that has overwhelmed her, the complete sense of worthlessness and loss:

> Naomi replied, "Turn back, my daughters. Why would you go with me? Will there again be sons in my womb, that they would be husbands for you? Turn back, my daughters. Go. I am too old for a husband. If I were to say that I have hope, even if I had a husband tonight, and even more, if I were to bear sons—would you wait

until they grew up? Would you refrain from having a husband? No, my daughters. This is more bitter for me than for you, since the LORD's will has come out against me."

Ruth refuses to leave her mother-in-law and we hear her crying out,

Don't urge me to abandon you, to turn back from following after you. Wherever you go, I will go; and wherever you stay, I will stay. Your people will be my people, and your God will be my God. Wherever you die, I will die, and there I will be buried. May the LORD do this to me and more so if even death separates me from you.

Together the two women journey back to Naomi's home community. Through a series of events, their hope is restored through prayers, a vision for a future, and action steps that Ruth takes in an effort to keep both of them alive. The beautiful story helps us discover how faith-filled people have a vision for their future. Out of their active love for God and for each other, they reclaim hope. A vision, a path, and responsive actions move them back to hope, which in turn leads to trust in themselves and trust in God.

Hope Restored: The Story of Job

The word *hope* occurs twenty-three times in the book of Job. The epilogue at Job 42 is often cited when moving from complex despair and hopelessness to renewed hope. Most are familiar with this story of a trustworthy man who is allowed to have his faithfulness tested by an adversary[8] and endures every kind of devastation, loss, disaster, and physical disease possible in an effort to destroy his hope so that he curses God.

In Job 4, after he experienced the loss of his children and is covered by disease from head to toe, he begins his lament. But he refuses to curse God. His friends show up, and one of them asserts that he has sinned and is therefore receiving these disastrous experiences as a consequence of his unfaithfulness.

---

8. Some translations equate this adversary with the devil, but the word in Hebrew refers to a heavenly being in the divine counsel.

Eliphaz of Teman responds to Job's lament:

If one tries to answer you, will you be annoyed?
But who can hold words back?
Look, you've instructed many
and given strength to drooping hands.
Your words have raised up the falling;
you've steadied failing knees.
But now it comes to you, and you are dismayed;
it has struck you, and you are frightened.
Isn't your religion the source of your confidence;
the integrity of your conduct, the source of your hope?
Think! What innocent person has ever perished?
When have those who do the right thing been destroyed?
As I've observed, those who plow sin and sow trouble will harvest it.
When God breathes deeply, they perish;
by a breath of his nostril they are annihilated. (Job 4:1-9)

The other twenty-two references to the word *hope* in Job point to the pure misery and hopelessness that Job experiences in this test before the adversary and God. At the end of this book,[9] when God finally responds to Job's lament, we discover that while God does not cause his misery, God uses this misery to strengthen and refine Job's character. Hope is restored to Job through God's faithful response. Job's response to God's vision becomes the blessing that leads him out of the depths of his despair. Again, there is a pattern for Job moving from sheer hopelessness to a vision for a different future, to restored confidence in God for his future. Job had hope that God is righteous and just. Job's hope led him to believe that there was more happening to him than he could even understand. And because of that hope, Job knew he must trust God, and God trusted Job to have hope in him, be faithful, and follow through on his love for God.

I sometimes feel as though I am in Job's story. My suffering has not been as extreme as Job's, but when I am falling into despair, I think

---

9. Most scholars think the ending or prologue was appended later to the poetry when this story entered the Hebrew Bible.

about Job. How does one not curse God while enduring the kind of travesties that Job faced? How does one hold on to hope, when disaster after disaster happens, and even your closest of friends question your behaviors and actions with respect to your faith? Job sometimes feels too close to life and too real for comfort.

This book of the Bible puts Job on trial, and it also puts God on trial because it tests our faith about the character of God and God's trust in us. Apparently God completely trusts in Job's faithfulness before allowing him to be questioned and challenged by the adversary. This intriguing story gives us a glimpse of God's character and God's trust in God's creation as God puts Job's hope on the line. It does make Christians stop and wonder.

From Despair to Real Hope: The Romans Story

The two Old Testament illustrations show ordinary faithful people living out their hope by trusting God and trusting each other. They move from despair to real hope. They aren't professional leaders in the church, such as clergy or priests. They are faithful followers of God.

As we turn to Romans, we discover leaders who imagine hope and communicate the need for trust in God, while acknowledging the real despair that exists in the human condition. The letter to the Jewish Christians in Rome contains a crucial teaching about the faithfulness of Jesus. John Wesley was listening to Martin Luther's preface to the book of Romans, at the Aldersgate church, when his heart was strangely warmed by the faithfulness of Jesus. Wesley later writes about the the design of God's grace in the book of Romans:

(Paul's) chief design herein is to show,

1.   That neither the gentiles by the law of nature, nor the Jews by the law of Moses, could obtain justification before God; and that therefore it was necessary for both to seek it from the free mercy of God by faith.

2. That God has an absolute right to show mercy on what terms he pleases, and to withhold it from those who will not accept it on his own terms.[10]

According to Wesley, Paul is trying to convince the Jewish Christians that they need to give up their conviction that they can earn salvation through their actions that justify their trust in God. Rather faith is a gift, which comes through unmerited grace and is granted to all of us because of God's incredible, faithful love for us. Because of that love, Jesus gave his life in sacrifice for all. Paul helps the Romans and the rest of us see that it is God's right to show mercy; it is not entitled because of our own actions or our will. Hope is present because we trust in Christ's faithfulness and thereafter can wholly trust in God's loyal love.

Paul explores God's righteousness evident through the witness of Jesus. He urges the Romans to claim the gospel for themselves, putting their whole trust in God: "I'm not ashamed of the gospel: it is God's own power for salvation to all who have faith in God, to the Jew first and also to the Greek. God's righteousness is being revealed in the gospel, from faithfulness for faith, as it is written, *The righteous person will live by faith*" (Rom 1:16-17).

He then chronicles how both Jews and Gentiles fall short of God's glory throughout history and into the current age. He soars into a speech about the deep chasm between God and humanity, because of the sinfulness of both the Jews and the Gentiles. And just when the reader believes that all hope for humanity is lost, Paul offers the saving pathway given to all through the life, death, and resurrection of Jesus.

But now God's righteousness has been revealed apart from the Law, which is confirmed by the Law and the Prophets. God's righteousness comes through the faithfulness of Jesus Christ for all who have faith in him. There's no distinction. All have sinned and fall short of God's glory, but all are treated as righteous freely

---

10. "Notes on St. Paul's Epistle to the Romans," Bible Study Tools, accessed May 10, 2017, http://www.biblestudytools.com/commentaries/wesleys-explanatory -notes/introductions/ro-intro.html.

by his grace because of a ransom that was paid by Christ Jesus. Through his faithfulness, God displayed Jesus as the place of sacrifice where mercy is found by means of his blood. He did this to demonstrate his righteousness in passing over sins that happened before, during the time of God's patient tolerance. He also did this to demonstrate that he is righteous in the present time, and to treat the one who has faith in Jesus as righteous. What happens to our bragging? It's thrown out. With which law? With what we have accomplished under the Law? No, not at all, but through the law of faith. We consider that a person is treated as righteous by faith, apart from what is accomplished under the Law. Or is God the God of Jews only? Isn't God the God of Gentiles also? Yes, God is also the God of Gentiles. Since God is one, then the one who makes the circumcised righteous by faith will also make the one who isn't circumcised righteous through faith. Do we then cancel the Law through this faith? Absolutely not! Instead, we confirm the Law. (Rom 3:21-31)

We have hope because God has hope in us. We trust God's trustworthy actions on the cross, which are evidence of God's desire to reach us. We trust God's righteousness because God offers us a pathway into a right relationship through Jesus Christ. Paul appeals for us to claim our hope in Christ through our faithful response. Therefore, the only decision to make is faithfulness, which is the source of our hope.[11]

It's All about Jesus

We can trust God through the life of Jesus as the Christ (Messiah) who brought hope for all who were lost and who are in need of a right relationship with God. The Gospels are filled with illustrations of the vision of God's kingdom that Jesus brought to those who heard him, followed him, and worship him. As we look at the need for hope in

---

11. Image Bearer, "N. T. Wright: Introduction to Romans," YouTube, April 27, 2016, https://youtu.be/wwtDUpWYEcY (start at 4:21). N. T. Wright reinforces this idea in his introduction to a Romans video where he states, "He [Paul] talks about the scriptures being given so that by the patience and study of these scriptures we might have hope, and that's of course where a lot of Romans is going."

order to build trust, we can turn to the Gospels and examine where Jesus brought hope to those who needed it the most. And through his invitation of hope, he communicated and confirmed that God is trustworthy and God is faithful. A quick examination of the Gospel of Mark will give us a glimpse of the vision Jesus offered the people about God and God's kingdom, the pathways he made clear for them to see where they needed to go to encounter God and deepen their relationship with God and the actions that Jesus himself took as an example of God's faithfulness in which hope can be grounded.

Mark

The Gospel of Mark offers readers a picture of Jesus that gives them hope. Mark was written to the people of Rome in a time and place where persecution and death were likely for early followers of Jesus. In the midst of that environment, Christians knew there was something worth living and dying for, so that their pain and suffering wasn't in vain. People needed hope. Mark 1:1-3 starts the Gospel with good news: "The beginning of the good news about Jesus Christ, God's Son, happened just as it was written about in the prophecy of Isaiah: *Look, I am sending my messenger before you. He will prepare your way, a voice shouting in the wilderness: 'Prepare the way for the Lord; make his paths straight.'*"

It's also good news that God hasn't forgotten them and that they aren't alone. He points to the work of John and then shares the anointing of Jesus as the Christ through the retelling of Jesus's baptism. Again, for the readers, it's a vision of God's promise being fulfilled, and it's a reminder that God is present and that God hears the cries of the people.

Next Mark 1:14-15 offers the pathway reinforced in the baptism narrative. "After John was arrested, Jesus came into Galilee announcing God's good news, saying, 'Now is the time! Here comes God's kingdom! Change your hearts and lives, and trust this good news!'" Jesus calls the first disciples who are drawn along with us into the story. Mark focuses on Jesus showing the people faithfulness every step of the way. He helps them see that God's work in this world doesn't look like what they expected it to look like. Instead Jesus builds their trust by showing them how to be caring, respectful, sincere, confident, and unselfish as he heals the sick, throws out demons, hangs out with the sinners, and demonstrates a life of piety without expecting recognition.

This pathway seems reasonable, right? The people in that time and place can be pious as they change their hearts and change their lives. But Mark then shows how following Jesus may mean going to the cross. Mark's Gospel prepares the reader for potential harassment, torture, and even death if they dare to live a transformed life in Christ. Their behaviors must be solidly grounded in hope that Jesus's words and God's promise will bring about their salvation. Mark literally shows them that Jesus cares and that Jesus has the authority to deliver on what God promised. Read Mark 4:35-41.

> Later that day, when evening came, Jesus said to them, "Let's cross over to the other side of the lake." They left the crowd and took him in the boat just as he was. Other boats followed along. Gale-force winds arose, and waves crashed against the boat so that the boat was swamped. But Jesus was in the rear of the boat, sleeping on a pillow. They woke him up and said, "Teacher, don't you care that we're drowning?" He got up and gave orders to the wind, and he said to the lake, "Silence! Be still!" The wind settled down and there was a great calm. Jesus asked them, "Why are you frightened? Don't you have faith yet?" Overcome with awe, they said to each other, "Who then is this? Even the wind and the sea obey him!"

Mark's Gospel illustrates the hope and the promise that people needed as they faced perils as followers in the early church. Trusting in Jesus meant taking a leap of faith that was reinforced by a sense of hope. Mark wanted to show them that those who walked with Jesus trusted him because he demonstrated that he was trustworthy through his words, his actions, and his authority. He cared for them, and this gave them hope.

The Hope Theory

Psychologist C. R. Snyder introduced the Hope Theory in 2002.[12] Snyder and his colleagues began thinking about hope and trying to define it in 1991. Collectively they define hope as "a positive motivational state that is based on an interactively derived sense of successful (a) agency (goal-directed energy), and (b) pathways (planning to meet goals)."[13] In his 2002 paper he uses this concept of a "trilogy" of thoughts and actions that make up the Hope Theory. Snyder argues that a person needs a goal (or vision) in order to cultivate and direct hope. Then they need to trust in certain pathways that will help them meet that goal (or vision). Finally, the person needs to be willing (or see themselves as willing) to take action toward that pathway in order to reach that goal (or vision). Hope is the "motivational state"[14] for this trilogy of thoughts, actions, and responses in the Hope Theory.

Snyder also asserts that hope is one of the ultimate ways in which we engage with other people to have better relationships. His research offers strong evidence that "high-hope" people are more willing to reach out to people when they themselves have a need or are trying to address certain needs:

> When encountering stressors, high-hope people can call on their family and friends—persons with whom they share a satisfying sense of mutuality. Higher hope is associated with better social adjustment, both with friends and one's extended family (Kwon, 2002). We have found that adults who are high in hope recount having close bonds to caregivers, along with large amounts of time spent with those caregivers (Rieger, 1993).[15]

---

12. C. R. Snyder, "Hope Theory: Rainbows in the Mind," *Psychological Inquiry*, vol. 13, no. 4 (2002): 249–75; accessed: October 1, 2017, http://www.jstor.org/stable/1448867.
13. Ibid., 287.
14. Ibid.
15. Ibid., 261.

Consider Erikson's earliest stages of development and the concept of trust versus mistrust that infants learn through their experiences with caregivers in their lives. Erikson's theory accompanies Snyder's argument that adults who are "high-hope people" can likely point to positive experiences that developed trust and a sense of self-worth in their early stages of life that contributes to their ability to trust.

If the care the infant receives is consistent, predictable, and reliable, they will develop a sense of trust that will carry with them to other relationships, and they will be able to feel secure even when threatened.

Success in this stage will lead to the virtue of hope. By developing a sense of trust, the infant can have hope that as new crises arise, there is a real possibility that other people will be there as a source of support.[16]

Take a look at people who are happy with their current careers and are hopeful about their futures. They can see clearly the goals and visions for their life or some aspect of their work. They also know what it's going to take to get them to that goal or vision for their future. They've got an idea what the path looks like to reach that desired place. With a goal or vision in mind and a pathway to get them there, people take action to move toward the goal. And with each step they take, their hope in themselves and in the possibility of achieving the final goal increases. They are willing to trust others more readily and are also willing to trust their own abilities to get them there. They are high-hope people.

Michael Phelps is the only Olympic athlete to earn twenty-eight Olympic gold medals. He is a renowned athlete who first tried to win an Olympic medal when he was fifteen years old.[17] He didn't earn the medal at the 2000 Olympics, but he met someone who had reached gold, and his hope began to rise for the future. As he observed and learned from Australian swimmer Ian Thorpe, he saw the pathway it

16. Saul McLeod, "Erik Erikson," *Simply Psychology*, published 2008, updated 2017, accessed April 10, 2017, https://www.simplypsychology.org/Erik-Erikson.html.
17. "Michael Phelps," Swim Swam, accessed May 10, 2017, https://swimswam.com/bio/michael-phelps/.

would take to get him to his goal. In one year at the World Championship Trials, he broke a world record that surpassed Ian Thorpe's record, and the Olympic medal was now in reach. By the 2004 Olympics, he was motivated to reach his goal and he had taken small strokes every day to get him to Athens, Greece. His hope was now within reach, and at the end of the Olympic Games, Phelps had six gold and two bronze medals to his name.[18]

It began with a hope that he could reach this goal as a child. Out of that hope he had to trust others and trust himself to get there. Hope sparks the fire that leads to the possibilities of our actions, which lead us to trust. Many other athletes inspire hope and trust.

Teachers are another example of everyday people who are high-hope people investing in the goal of educating our children and youth. As educators, they have hope that the children they are pouring their lives into every day will eventually become well-equipped, functioning adults who are helping make the world a better place. When I was in youth ministry, I engaged with teachers quite often as we partnered in aiming for this goal. I could see how another teacher's faith influenced her life in her classroom. Because she trusted God to do something valuable with her life, she had hope that her goal of helping young people was a goal worth pursuing. With that desire, she got up every day and got to work to design the pathways that would get her to this vision for her own life and the vision for the lives of these youth. She shared with me that the greatest reward in teaching is to have a former student come back to visit after graduation. Through that experience, she saw the kind of people they became as faithful adults, who are filled with hope for their future and a vision for how they will get there. These seeds of hope are planted by the power of the Holy Spirit, nurtured by the scriptural witness, and reinforced by the stories people tell as they learn to trust God, trust one another, and trust themselves because of that hope.

---

18. Ibid.

Trust → Hope

The development of relational trust based on hope is hard work. We want something, some outcome, some vision or some goal, so that we believe in ourselves and others if we can reliably achieve the outcome, vision, or goal. The Bible stories and our stories provide sufficient examples of where well-placed hope moved us into trust.

As faithful people, we articulate and acknowledge that every day when we live in hope we will be granted another day to trust by God's grace. Hope gives us the motivation that we need to encounter and engage with people on the mission field, where we desire good for all God's children. If hope is well formed, then every person you or I meet is potentially an authentically genuine person whom you or I can trust. Without a sense of hope, we wouldn't be willing to operate in a world where trust is needed in every transaction we make. I have confidence that the plane I get on is being piloted by an authentic, trained pilot who cares enough about passengers to take the extra precautions necessary to ensure our safe arrival. By getting on the plane, I'm trusting the pilot with my life. Based on hope, I trust that the work I do is actually helping people, most of whom I will never meet, to live better lives. Every day, based in hope, I trust coworkers to carry out their role and responsibilities with me as we serve the churches. We may have different ideas about how to carry out that work, but we all share the same hope. My actions originate out of my hope. And my hope is motivated by the goal of reaching and walking with God's people as they deepen their relationship with Christ. Hope is strengthened through the pathways we develop, and it is reinforced by a willingness to take action each and every day. In the biblical examples of hope from the Old and New Testament, each character had hope because God gave a vision or goal. Then God showed or provided the pathway to reach that vision or goal. Next God invited them to take action, which resulted in a faithful response once God made the first move. The stories begin and often end with hope for the unforeseen future, but the hope is experienced in the present even if the evidence for it seemed unobtainable. These biblical stories then point to God's trustworthiness because our ultimate source of hope is from God.

Goals and the vision for the future are the first stepping-stones guiding us deeper into trust. With that goal or vision articulated, we start searching for pathways to get us there. If the pathways are reasonable, achievable, and often affected by timing, confidence is nurtured, strengthened, and reinforced. With a clear map, hope inspires trust that with my own agency, and with the willingness of others to work with me, this map can and will become reality. I trust myself and I trust others and I trust God to help me reach the destination because I have hope that is grounded by trusting in the faithfulness of Jesus Christ.

God's relationship with people through the gift of hope is important to building trust. If we don't have hope in the future of humanity or in our mission, then it is less likely that we will trust one another. Because of hope in God, we keep coming back to trust over and over and over again, even when trust is broken, destroyed, or divested. Of course, we don't trust blindly or go into abusive and dangerous relationships that are obviously not trustworthy. Trust is built up in layers, with appropriate amounts of trust granted through layered relationships. But our hope is grounded in the way that God made us for relationship. We are called to stay in love with God and our neighbors, which requires us to keep coming back and finding ways to build trust, communicate trust, and inspire trust. Without God's beautiful design for trust, the world would not be able to operate. All things are possible when you have hope!

Questions to Consider

1. What are some examples of a goal you had where you saw a path and took a leap of faith to trust someone or some group?

2. What happened in that experience? Did you achieve your goal?

3. Can you describe the pathways that brought you to that goal and what actions you needed to take to reach that goal?

Chapter 3

4. Who else had to see the hope in your vision to help you carry it out?

5. Were there biblical passages that helped strengthen that hope?

6. What other biblical passages reinforce the gift of hope and help you take steps toward trust?

Chapter 4
Trust → Love

L ove makes the world go around."[1] If trust is needed and practiced 24/7/365 days a year, then love and trust work hand-in-hand for all human relationships. We build trust because we love. Love what? Well, that's the question, because there are many things that we love that cause us to take actions, react to actions, and avoid actions. And there are many ways to define and describe love. Love can be a noun or a verb. Love can be felt and experienced in a myriad of ways. As a noun, it is "a strong affection for another arising out of kinship or personal ties, an unselfish loyal and benevolent concern for the good of another."[2] Love can be beautiful when placed on the right things and the right people for the right reasons. Love based on selfish desire can also be misplaced, abandoned, and exchanged, which can cause anger, frustration, and disasters that destroy communities, neighborhoods, businesses, and people. Healthy love leads to productive trust.

Many books about love are available from psychological, sociological, and theological domains. In this chapter we will narrow the scope by looking at the theological understanding of *agape* love, which might be called godly love. It is love based on *brotherly love, affection, good*

---

1. An idiom often used in common language. Recently the phrase was turned into a song by Jennifer Lopez and Lin-Manuel Miranda as a tribute to the victims of the 2016 nightclub shooting in Orlando.
2. "Love," Definition of Love, accessed June 9, 2017, https://www.merriam -webster.com/dictionary/love.

will, benevolence,[3] which cause us to be willing to sacrifice our own self-interests and motivations for the sake of others.

Failure to Love

Godly love has fallen by the wayside in the global milieu of the twenty-first century. An emphasis on individual identity and economic transaction makes agape love more and more difficult. We must "get something in return" for us to do something for others, for another cause, or for the good of the whole. This is one reason why we have lost trust in our institutions, because we have lost our loyal love for what our communities stand for and what we are fighting for in the communities where we "serve." Simultaneously, institutions have also forgotten and taken for granted what they stand for and whom they love.

For example, Barack Obama, in his presidential farewell speech, tried to remind the people what we love about being citizens. He appealed to our distinct identity as a democracy that stands for the people, by the people. He said,

> That's what I want to focus on tonight: The state of our democracy. Understand, democracy does not require uniformity. Our founders argued. They quarreled. Eventually they compromised. They expected us to do the same. But they knew that democracy does require a basic sense of solidarity—the idea that for all our outward differences, we're all in this together; that we rise or fall as one.[4]

His invitation reminds us that we love the ideal that every citizen has the opportunity to influence the future, to change our current situations, and to join others in shaping our communities and our homes. He urged citizens to fall in love with the ideals that define their country. Unfortunately, divisions of power, economic disparities, and attitudes of distrust

---

3. Ibid.
4. Barack Obama, "President Obama's Farewell Address: Full Text," *CNN Politics,* January 11, 2017, http://www.cnn.com/2017/01/10/politics/president-obama-farewell-speech/.

have caused deep fissures in our societies. Our love for humanity has dwindled and our love for neighbor is challenged. We have such a hard time setting aside our differences that we can barely acknowledge the humanity in the people we have "othered."[5] If you were to judge how people treat one another based upon what you read in social media, you know what this means. We abandon common courtesy and human dignity by demonizing people we don't agree with, people we don't understand, and people we perceive to be our enemies. We cannot and should not demonize leaders just because we don't agree. We must find a way to trust God and neighbor even in the midst of anger, frustration, and fear. Therefore, staying in love with God and with our neighbors created by God means that we must find a way forward, trusting in God's whole grace.

Failure to Love in the Church

The most alarming place where we have failed to love is in our Christian communities. The divisions within our congregations and throughout our denominations are very deep. We have fallen out of love with one another, so that our differences dominate our conversations, our attitudes, and our behaviors. Many of the Protestant churches once again are broken by schism and disunity.

I travel among leaders throughout my denomination. I'm highly discouraged by the rhetoric of distrust, frustration, and angst that fuels hopelessness and seems to be leading to separation. We can no longer live with our differences, we think, so it is easier to separate ourselves from these differences by metaphorically and literally departing from one another. For some, departing from one another in our connection is driven by social and theological convictions about the practice of same-gender marriage or ordination for clergy in a same-gender marriage. For

---

5. This term is a way of describing how we create and magnify differences by "othering" people who don't think like us, act like us, or look like us. There is research and interest in this concept in sociological studies and theological studies. You can read more about "othering" at https://othersociologist.com/otherness -resources/. For a theological analysis see William H. Willimon, *Fear of the Other* (Nashville: Abingdon, 2016).

others, the divorce might be driven by deeper disagreement about the practices of biblical interpretation. Because of this impasse, some of us no longer want to be known as members of the same faith community.

Adding to the complexity of this divide is a generation of leaders who feel that they have been disagreeing for too long. Most younger leaders want to keep trying to find a way to live together in spite of our differences.

A number of complex factors make the decision to separate difficult. Amongst those factors are ownership of property, an employer-employee relationship, financial resources, and many other assets that depend on mutual and sacred trust. How do we untangle attitudes and beliefs from the real-life division of property, resources, and other assets? Our love for our own holiness and righteousness wins out over our love for each other, which in turn has caused us to distrust one another and the institution that once held us together in hope for transformation of the world.

Throughout the history of my Methodist denomination, and since the wisdom received from Francis Asbury about the *Causes, Evils, and Cures of Church and Heart Divisions,*[6] we've emphasized love more than right opinion and stood together with hope and in confidence that our differences could be overcome. We affirm this beautiful vision of the body of Christ that seeks to be together, to love one another as examples of "agape love," which Christ demonstrated through his life, death, and resurrection. We love this ideal and we want to live into this ideal. We believed this ideal can be truly reached and embodied.

Even with this ideal for godly love, other desires arise and caucuses emerge around different values, which give groups secondary identities within the uniting identity of the denomination. Caucuses form around ethnic diversity, theological diversity, and cultural diversity. Soon, the caucus positions win the loyal love of their followers more than the godly love that defines the identity that created the relationship in a denomination with a common purpose. Caucuses can be useful for lifting up groups who

---

6. First published in 1792, reissued on the eve of the split between the Northern and Southern Methodists over slavery, and reissued again in abridged form in 2016 by Abingdon Press.

are excluded or marginalized. But the loyal love is lost when caucus ideals tear people away from each other rather than help strengthen, refine, and improve the godly love present in the whole. The love for the whole church and the mission field can be lost when more love is granted to our fragmented and individualized ideals. Without our loyal and faithful love that binds us together, trust is gone and the church loses its unity because of our diversity on issues we believe are irreconcilable. Sadly, division frays the beautiful design of God's creation, which is the body of Christ.

The Loss of Love and Trust Hurts

As human beings in relationship, we all have known the loss of love and the loss of trust. It hurts. No matter who you are or where you are, this kind of loss leaves broken relationships, diminished resources, and ineffective impact for mission and ministry in the world. Whenever churches split around ideology, we damage Christ's witness in the world. Our actions tell the world that it's easier and more acceptable to walk away from one another and abandon one another when we don't see things eye to eye. It is much easier to walk away from one another when we allow our anger and our divisions to drive a wedge between our relationships. It is much more difficult to stay and engage with one another and keep working on the relationship than it is to leave because we refuse to do the hard work of figuring it out. We "fall out of love" and embrace the "it's too hard" narrative.

You know this narrative. It's often the language used when we see a marriage falling apart. "It's too hard to talk to him." "She doesn't see my point of view." "He will never change his mind." "I just don't love you anymore." This abdication reflects the limitations of human thinking and disregards the power of God's love for us. We are sinful, fallen, limited human beings who fall prey to our own limited imaginations. Our problem is that we allow the human limitations of love to be reflected in the church, where we are supposed to allow the unlimited, unconditional understanding of God to be the reflection of love. In reality, love is hard. Life is hard, and trust takes a lot of hard work. How do we become better witnesses of God's love by enduring through the difficulties of human diversity? The church's witness matters.

If the church can show how to live with one another and love one another in the midst of deeply rooted, sometimes painful diversities, then the world can see how faith and trust and hope can be God's gift for human flourishing around the world. If the church can challenge people to live with integrity, so that they can be known as trustworthy and loving to others, then we pour a little bit more goodness and hope into the cultural landscape of the world. If the church can shape people's lives by teaching them humility and grace, then there will be fewer people concerned with having the right opinion and more people concerned with sharing God's love. How will we do that? Is it really feasible to get to live with God's love and to share it with the world? How difficult is it to live with love as the guiding value for building trust? The Bible shows us how God's love leads to greater trust.

The "Trust Stack" in the Bible

Rachel Botsman's concept of the "Trust Stack" helps us reflect on the biblical interpretation of God's love. If love leads to trust, then there are some features of God's love that build the trust that binds Christians together. Botsman defines trust as "a confident relationship that leads to the unknown."[7] She suggests that trust comes when people take steps to engage in a series of ideas and actions that lead to risking trust. Her research into the concept of collaborative consumption shows that technology changes how we engage in an economy of trust. People "climb the trust stack," when we

1. trust the idea;

2. trust or have confidence in the platform; and

---

7. Rachel Botsman, "We've Stopped Trusting Institutions and Started Trusting Strangers," TEDSummit, June 2016, https://www.ted.com/talks/rachel_botsman _we_ve_stopped_trusting_institutions_and_started_trusting_strangers?utm _source=tedcomshare&utm_medium=referral&utm_campaign=tedspread.

3. use little bits of information to decide whether the other person (or institution) is trustworthy.[8]

Botsman assesses the trust disruptions that occurred in society over several hundred years.

This "trust stack" concept can help us interpret some key stories in the Bible. God built trust by illustrating God's faithfulness through the covenant of love.

God's Love Leads to Trust in the Old Testament

The Old Testament offers significant information toward God's character. Many stories reveal the human condition and who God is in relation to humanity. It's our guide to how deep and wide God's love for creation is in spite of repeated human failures.

Genesis: Trust the Idea

God's love is apparent through divine interaction with God's creation. God is the subject of Genesis 1. God is the creator who made all things in this world, from the sun and the moon, to the stars in the sky. The primary conclusion, which God alone renders, is that God's creation is good.

When God began to create the heavens and the earth—the earth was without shape or form, it was dark over the deep sea, and God's wind swept over the waters—God said, "Let there be light." And so light appeared. God saw how good the light was. God separated the light from the darkness. God named the light Day and the darkness Night. There was evening and there was morning: the first day.

God said, "Let there be a dome in the middle of the waters to separate the waters from each other." God made the dome and

---

8. Rachel Botsman, "The Changing Rules of Trust in the Digital Age," *Harvard Business Review* (October 20, 2015).

separated the waters under the dome from the waters above the dome. And it happened in that way. God named the dome Sky.

There was evening and there was morning: the second day.

God said, "Let the waters under the sky come together into one place so that the dry land can appear." And that's what happened. God named the dry land Earth, and he named the gathered waters Seas. God saw how good it was. God said, "Let the earth grow plant life: plants yielding seeds and fruit trees bearing fruit with seeds inside it, each according to its kind throughout the earth." And that's what happened. The earth produced plant life: plants yielding seeds, each according to its kind, and trees bearing fruit with seeds inside it, each according to its kind. God saw how good it was.

The phrase "God saw how good it was" appears in the first creation story six times, one pronouncement for each day, and the last assessment is superlative: "God saw everything he had made: it was supremely good!" (Gen 1:31). Our introduction to the creator overflows with the love that the creator has for the created. The idea, the first stage of trust, is that the creation is good, beautiful, worthy of God's attention and affection. The object of this affection is creation, and the subject (the creator) returns this love.

Love seems to be an innate part of our human condition. The desire to love and be loved is the original idea that draws us into trusting the Genesis story. We take the first step on the trust stack by affirming the idea that God loves what God creates. Since God takes the first step of love, it's an idea we want to believe.

Genesis: Trust the Platform

The Israelite audience for the creation story would have heard these words with a polytheistic, mythical, cultural imagination. Their interpretation of the creation story points to the devolution of the world, which emerges from a perfectly created wonder, in which they discover the pains of trying to return to that perfect state. For those living through disasters, challenges, and wars that constantly threaten life and well-being, to imagine themselves as part of something "good" must have been very hopeful. Despite evidence to the contrary, they trust the idea that the creator intends a good creation and that they themselves as a part of creation are good. If a human being knows that their creation is "good," they can trust that they are loved and worthy of love. The priests who told the creation story, as a way to worship God, built the foundation of trust in God by communicating that God meets the human need for goodness (moral beauty) and love. The second step in the trust stack was taken onto the platform and strengthened through the desire and experience of God's love.

Genesis: Trust the Bits and Pieces of Information

The next step in the trust stack is to take pieces of information to decide whether a person or institution is trustworthy. In Genesis the authors convey that humanity is created in the image of God. Authority is established because of one's proximity to the divine:

> In Mesopotamia, a significance of the image can be seen in the practice of kings setting up images of themselves in places where they want to establish their authority. Other than that, it is only other gods who are made in the image of gods. Thus, their traditions speak of sons being in the image of their fathers but not of human beings created in the image of God.[9]

If this parallel to imagery for ancient kings is accurate, and if the early Israelites associated their created image with the divine, they too would be associated with God's power and authority, which gives them the freedom to change their outcome. Most scholars think the first creation story reached written form during the Israelite exile, when God's people were separated from their homes and neighbors and when trust in God's covenant appeared to be lost. If they could see the image of God in themselves, then maybe they could be as loving and as loved as their creator. By remembering the goodness of God's creation, despite

---

9. John H. Walton, "Summary Overview of Genesis 1:1-2:3," *The NIV Application Commentary: Genesis* (Grand Rapids: Zondervan, 2011).

loss and suffering, God's people could once again imagine and experience a God who is loving and caring. If the creator could put such detail and care into the beauty of the pristine world, they could trust the creator who designed humanity to inhabit the same love and care within.

Numerous other stories in the Old Testament test the "trust stack" concept. More than 150 passages or sayings in the Old Testament[10] call for trust in God and trustworthiness among God's people. Trust is based in faithfulness to God, and it builds a platform that often weaves trusted groups and systems into the foundation of Israelite life.

God's Love Leads to Trust in the New Testament

The New Testament invites us to consider how God's love stays constant in the midst of cultural, social changes in the world. Having moved from understanding love through the boundaries that are designed to protect people in the Old Testament, the New Testament gives us a whole new understanding of unconditional love discovered through the life, death, and resurrection of Jesus. With that in mind, we'll turn to the Gospel of Mark.

Mark: Trust the Idea

We focus on Mark, which is known as the older Gospel used in writing the Gospels of Matthew and Luke. *Euangelion* is the Greek word for gospel.[11] When I was in youth ministry, I loved teaching about a gospel and inviting the students to discover and learn more about this fully loaded word. There are many ways to translate this term. Common phrases include: "the good news," "a good message,"

10. Bible Gateway, accessed May 10, 2017, https://www.biblegateway.com/quicksearch/?quicksearch=trust&qs_version=CEB.

11. εὐαγγέλιον euangélion, yoo-ang-ghel'-ee-on; from the same as G2097; a good message, i.e., the gospel: Blue Letter Bible, accessed January 27, 2017, https://www.blueletterbible.org/lang/lexicon/lexicon.cfm?t=kjv&strongs=g2098.

"good tidings," or "glad tidings," and "the proclamation of the grace of God manifest and pledged in Christ."[12] The opening sentence in the Gospel of Mark prefers "good news."

> The beginning of the good news about Jesus Christ, God's Son, happened just as it was written about in the prophecy of Isaiah:
>
> Look, I am sending my messenger before you.
>
> > He will prepare your way,
> > a voice shouting in the wilderness:
> > "Prepare the way for the Lord;
> > make his paths straight." (Mark 1:1-3)

Mark begins with the idea that there is good news concerning this person named Jesus. What John the Baptist was proclaiming was directly tied to their history and the words of the ancient prophets. The people in that time and place needed an idea, a thought that was different than the doom and gloom they were experiencing in the world of the Roman Empire. They needed to know that God hadn't completely abandoned them and that life could only get better than what they were experiencing at present. They were doing their best to trust God through their practices, their faithfulness, and even their love for one another, but things didn't seem to be getting easier. Any good news would be a welcomed idea; it resonates with their desires.

Mark: Trust the Platform

The primary platform for the delivery of the good news about Jesus is John the Baptist. The Gospel introduces us to John immediately as a trusted, apocalyptic preacher who points to the end times while paving the path for the coming Christ. Why did people trust John as the platform for this message?

Let's unpack what made John the Baptist the trusted source for delivering God's love through Jesus. In order to piece together our understanding of John the Baptist, most biblical scholars examine the

---

12. Ibid.

Gospels and supplement this record with the Jewish historian Flavius Josephus, who lived between 37 CE and approximately 100 CE.[13] The biblical platform portrays him as a prominent character tied to Jesus in each Gospel. He is an eclectic outsider who draws the attention of the people through his preaching and through his behaviors. "John wore clothes made of camel's hair, with a leather belt around his waist. He ate locusts and wild honey" (Mark 1:6). His words and ideas, noted as the first step on the trust stack, were drawing crowds and the attention of other authorities. John drew so much attention that he was arrested and eventually killed by Herod Antipas. But Herod couldn't kill him right away because of his popularity (Matt 14:5).

Another part of John's appeal is his ability to use the scriptural platform of trust. He used the prophet Isaiah to speak about the coming of Jesus, and he used Jesus's Jewish identity and the language relevant to the people in early Judaism. With a deep sense of humility, he pointed to the future as he spoke. "One stronger than I am is coming after me. I'm not even worthy to bend over and loosen the strap of his sandals. I baptize you with water, but he will baptize you with the Holy Spirit" (Mark 1:7-8). He gained authority and trust among the people by using the practices and rituals of purification that were familiar to them, adding a different dimension to the interpretation of this practice.

> John the Baptist, of course, is known for having practiced baptism. But then, so did lots of other people. We hear of other groups around this time, besides the Sadducees and the Pharisees and Essenes. There are the obscure little groups. We only know their names, but one of them is called Morning Dippers, or Hemero-Baptists, they're called. This seems to refer to a group that practiced self-washing...ritual washing as an act of purification. We also know from the Dead Sea Scrolls, that the Qumran community practiced ritual washing as an act of purification as well, to keep themselves pure before God. So, the idea of baptizing or washing as

---

13.   G. J. Goldberg, editor, The Flavius Josephus Home Page, accessed January 27, 2017, http://josephus.org/.

a sign of purity seems to come, actually, out of the Temple practice itself.[14]

The ritual practices of the culture gave authority to John's platform, which established trust. The trust for Jesus increased because the people believed in the lineage of wisdom conveyed by the early prophets and strengthened by John the Baptist.

Mark: Trust the Bits and Pieces of Information

Despite writing the shortest Gospel in the New Testament, the author of Mark wove together bits and pieces of Jesus's life in such a way that brought hope to the people in that time and place. Reading and hearing the good news is effective in a context where life wasn't always easy, and the persecutions experienced in the Greco-Roman Empire instilled more fear in the people than hope. The bits and pieces, the sayings, of Jesus's life story flow through the Gospel of Mark. From the tempting of Jesus to the call of the disciples, Jesus didn't fit the mold of typical men in his time and place. People were likely intrigued by this son of a carpenter who began to do things a little differently. Imagine walking alongside the Galilee Sea and all of the sudden some guy calls out to you while you are fishing and says, "Come, follow me, . . . and I'll show you how to fish for people" (Mark 1:17). Their trust ultimately led to love, but novelty of the call enhanced the curiosity about this man named Jesus. The other bit of information that drew people into this story are the responses of the first disciples. They were ordinary men who fit the norms of the society and culture and yet, when called to follow Jesus, they took substantial risks by leaving everything they knew and everything they loved, trusting this man to lead them to a changed heart and a new life. If these ordinary guys were willing to do something so significantly different with their lives, then perhaps an ordinary person like myself could also find transformation through this love of God.

14. L. Michael White, "John the Baptist," PBS, April 1998, http://www.pbs.org/wgbh/pages/frontline/shows/religion/portrait/john.html.

The Gospel of Mark contains many stories of Jesus breaking the rules and challenging the regime, doing miracles and sharing parables. Each story gives the people another glimpse of a piece of Jesus's life. And throughout the tapestry of this beautiful design, you can see people melting as they fall in love with this man who shows the love of God in ways no one had ever seen before. As Christians, we learn to love God because of the life, death, and resurrection of Jesus, the risen Christ. Enough of the biographical bits and pieces of information are arranged in the Gospels that people willingly trust someone who lived more than two thousand years ago. We are persuaded that he is Christ, God's Son. We trust Jesus's love so much that our hope expects nothing less than everlasting life.

This vision of godly love has transformed millions of people's lives over thousands of years. It has inspired people to do things they wouldn't normally do and trust people they wouldn't normally trust. This idea of agape love catapults people from a self-oriented way of being into a selfless standard of living that challenges any design humanity could ever create. In that time and place and even today, the love of God disrupted and disrupts the ways in which people live their lives and learn to trust.

Agape Love Makes You Do Crazy Things

In the twenty-first century agape love can make people do some crazy things. Through God's love for every human being, we are invited to set aside our own well-being for the greater good of others. It is very difficult to find our way into this kind of unconditional love, in which we are willing to give up our very lives so that others can live. But people do it every day. This is possible because of the Imago Dei that lives within us, whether we acknowledge it or not. Wesleyans call that prevenient grace. This kind of grace drives the good that we do before we even recognize that this goodness came from the creator as a gift with no expectations in return. Agape love is an unconditional love for all of creation.

There are also layers of agape love lived out by our fellow humans in a multitude of different ways. For example, there must be love for humanity that police officers and firefighters have within to put their lives at risk for others. It is not an easy job, nor is it glamorous, but for those who carry this calling with the best intentions in mind, they are living out the beautiful design of love of neighbor, which is founded in trust.

In July 2016, protestors took to the streets of Dallas to bring attention to the discrimination against black men and women by some law enforcement officers in many cities across the United States. The Dallas police officers were there to ensure that the protest was safe for participants and safe for observers. In the midst of this peaceful protest, violence broke out when a single shooter opened fire at the officers and the crowd. According to the *Washington Post*, "Images and video show officers pulling fallen comrades out of harm's way, of officers 'running toward gunfire, from an elevated position, with no chance to protect themselves and to put themselves in harm's way, to make sure citizens can get to a place of security,' Dallas Police Chief David Brown said."[15]

Four police officers and one Dallas Area Rapid Transit officer gave their lives for others that day by showing what real sacrificial love for humanity looks like. This kind of sacrificial love for others that the Dallas police officers demonstrated grew the trust of the Dallas citizens, including the protestors, as they sought ways to do better together for the sake of the Dallas community.

Consider the firefighters and rescue workers who lost their lives during the terror attacks in New York on September 11, 2001. Think about the soldiers and heroic civilians who willingly put their lives in danger so that the freedom of others can be experienced and honored. We may not know each person individually, but we know what they stand for, and our trust grows when they demonstrate their love for us through their work of service for the greater good.

15. Elahe Izadi, "How Police Officers Protected Black Lives Matter Protesters during Dallas Shooting," *The Washington Post,* July 8, 2016, https://www.washingtonpost.com/news/inspired-life/wp/2016/07/08/the-acts-of-heroism-during-a-deadly-night-in-dallas/?utm_term=.9806d213b02f.

Disruptions in Trust through Love

Rachel Botsman startled us by making the claim that we are willing to trust strangers more than institutions. Let's test Botsman's "trust stack" concept with our understanding of faithful love that is being challenged by technology. Just as technology is changing our ways of engaging one another and learning from one another, so it is also changing our ways of processing information and establishing opinions. It changes how we conceive of love for neighbors and love for others. Technology can bring out the best in us and the worst in us when it disrupts our mutual trust.

Examining Trust through Love

In many ways, social media changes how we see one another. For example, a statistical analysis of men actively engaged in the lives of their young children shows that a high percentage of black or African American men are not living with their children.[16] This data reinforced myths about black men's absence in the lives of their offspring. But through social media, we get to see, experience, and empathize with complete strangers in ways never imagined, and this challenges our statistical conclusions. People give us a glimpse of their souls by displaying intimate moments of their lives and their children's lives. For example, in a video of a black man with his four-year-old daughter, he has her repeat after him in the bathroom mirror:

He says, "I am strong," and she repeats, "I am strong!"
Followed by "I am smart."
Then "I work hard."

16. Jo Jones and William D. Mosher, "Fathers Involvement with their Children: United States 2006–2010," December 20, 2013, National Health Statistics Report, https://www.cdc.gov/nchs/data/nhsr/nhsr071.pdf, p. 12.

"I am beautiful."

"I am respectful," which she repeats, "I am *refectful.*"

"I am not better than anyone."

"Nobody's better than me."

"I am amazing."

"I am great."

"I am blessed."[17]

If you have preconceived negative notions about how a black man parents his daughter, this video challenges those conceptions. You begin to see things from a different point of view. The idea that parental love looks different when faced with a diversity of challenges is now within your reach. You don't necessarily have to know this family, but the video platform draws this man and his daughter closer to your particular life than ever before possible. Piecing this information with your own experiences begins to change your thinking and maybe even your concepts about trusting black men. Seeing humanity love one another through social media invites us to explore love of humanity a little more than we previously realized. This is why Botsman believes we are more willing to trust strangers than we are institutions, because strangers feel much closer when we have access to their lives through technologies that bridge distance. Institutions still feel distant, because they have lost the human touch and have disconnected their purpose from the human love that builds trust. Institutions have also not discovered how to use technology to communicate their love for humanity. Instead, we see government institutions and bureaucracies using technology to defend policies and justify opinions. The more likes or followers one has, the more value is given to popular opinion versus human empathy.

17. USA Today, "Dad and Daughter Inspire with Morning Affirmations," September 22, 2016, https://youtu.be/zNtPVgblzWY.

Devaluation of Human Love

Concerns are rising throughout the world about the devaluation of human lives. Because trust is so low across humanity, we are hardened toward people in real need, seeking shelter, seeking compassion, seeking safety for themselves and their children. The worldwide waves of global migration puts millions of refugees in search of countries willing to give them asylum and allow them to live without fear. But because trust is so low, some countries are refusing to allow refugees into the country and finding ways to limit immigration. One tweet stated, "I can't understand the heart that doesn't shatter at the sight of children in a boat on the sea wearing toy floaties."[18] She was responding to an order to ban refugees from any part of the world and build a wall against illegal immigrants from Mexico. She was bemoaning the loss of love for our neighbors. She and many others via social media are crying out against the seemingly stringent laws that are being instituted at the expense of human lives.

On the other hand, the proponents of these laws feel bound to protect the lives of the people already within the country. They are crying out against violent acts that are attributed to extremists among various religious sects. Their rhetoric escalates the fear of others to new levels. The extreme spokesmen set up camp and dig their stakes deep into the ground. There is no trust for the other and no love lost between the ideologues who believe that their position holds the corner on truth. Trust seems gone, and love for humanity appears to be wavering.

Where Is the Love?

In the current cultural landscape, it's easy to throw your hands up and want to give up. It's easy to find a cave and hide from all people because you feel as though you can't trust anyone. It's easy to lose hope that agape love may prevail because it feels so far away and so impossible for anyone to embrace. Can we or will we ever change our minds to see the other person's point of view? Can we or will we ever find ways to trust

---

18. Tweeted by All in All @carissalynn on January 26, 2017.

again? Or will we live in fear of the unknown, in fear of the "other," and seek asylum from humanity?

No doubt God has felt this way throughout time as our creator watched humanity destroy one another, turn back to selfish ways, and deny or devastate creation. And yet one biblical story after another points to the God who never gives up on creation. We fall short of the creator's expectations and yet the creator forgives, offers unmerited grace, and trusts us again, wooing us to choose love for one another so that we might be able to trust one another again.

Rachel Botsman talks about the disruptions in the cultural norms of the fabric of trust. She argues that

> what we cannot deny is that the way trust flows through society is changing, and it's creating this big shift away from the 20th century that was defined by institutional trust towards the 21st century that will be fueled by distributed trust. Trust is no longer top-down. It's being unbundled and inverted. It's no longer opaque and linear. A new recipe for trust is emerging that once again is distributed amongst people and is accountability-based.[19]

I believe that God's vision for trust was always "unbundled and inverted." Creation is structured in such a way that we would discover how much we need one another to survive and thrive. Trust must be distributed, networked, and carefully woven together into magnificent pieces of art that reinforce our awe of God's creation. It can be beautiful when love leads to trust.

Extreme Love for Neighbor

Thirty-one-year-old Chris Salvatore and eighty-nine-year-old Norma Patavina came into an unlikely friendship in 2013. As they got to know each other their friendship grew and then Norma was diagnosed

---

19. Rachel Botsman, "We've Stopped Trusting Institutions and Started Trusting Strangers," TEDSummit, June 2016, https://www.ted.com/talks/rachel_botsman _we_ve_stopped_trusting_institutions_and_started_trusting_strangers?utm _source=tedcomshare&utm_medium=referral&utm_campaign=tedspread.

with leukemia. She was in need of constant care, but couldn't afford it. So Chris created a GoFundMe account and helped Norma raise money to receive the care she needed as her health continued to decline. When the money ran out, Chris invited her into his home. With Norma having no family and Chris adoring Norma, they became roommates of another kind. Chris sacrificed his own comfort and freedom to care for Norma, and Norma loves Chris like her own grandson. This is a worthy example of agape love that grew into a deep and profound trust of one another to care for neighbor beyond either of their imaginations. In an interview with NBC News, Chris states, "As much as I'm here helping her, she's helped me tremendously. She has really brought me back to what's important. Family, love, human kindness." As the interviewer ended the story, he noted that this is "the bond of a lifetime and the true meaning of love thy neighbor." Chris epitomized love for humanity that manifested itself in his love for Norma. It is possible. It can be done.[20]

Questions to Consider

1. Where have you experienced love that led to a deep and profound trust between you and other people?

2. Where have you witnessed love that led to trust in your family, your work environment, your church, or your community?

3. What other scriptures illustrate this love of God that led to people ultimately believing and trusting in God's promises?

4. Out of those scriptures, which sayings or stories resonate with your life in this current moment?

5. Have there ever been moments when you felt as though you lost love for humanity and therefore lost your trust in the human race? What may have caused that and how did you turn around?

---

20. Lester Holt, NBC Nightly News, *Inspiring America,* January 2017.

Designed to Forgive

But It's Sooo Hard...

I f you have ever experienced broken trust, you know how painful and devastating it can be. Among intimate relationships, infidelity in a marriage can ruin the people involved. It can make you doubt yourself, doubt your partner, and even doubt the people around you as you wonder who knew and didn't say anything to you. Broken trust in working relationships can be just as devastating. When you thought someone had your back and was supportive of you and your work and later you discover they did something to undermine you or blame you, this can ruin your confidence and damage your faith in your coworkers and your hope for good working relationships. The loss of trust can destroy workplaces.

I am guilty of seeking consolation among colleagues and friends who will "see my side," when trust has been broken in my life. I am guilty of ignoring, avoiding, and even letting go of relationships and friendships because I experienced a deep fissure in the finely woven trust of our community. When I experience broken trust, I am often so hurt that I want little to do with the person or the institution that caused my pain. In reality, broken trust can create a chasm so deep and wide it's difficult to see any possibility for reconciliation. Broken trust can lead to wars, rigidity in laws, and institutional disintegration.

Trust is critical, and when it is shattered, it seems impossible to trust again.

And yet we are called, invited, and compelled to find ways to trust and to continue to be trustworthy people. To live in a world where you trust no one leaves you isolated and always living in fear. To live where you are typically second-guessing the people around you because you are weary of trusting anyone, makes it hard for others to let their guard down around you. When you don't have trust in your relationships, whether intimate or working, it can lead you to do things you wouldn't normally do. Trust must be extended and trust must be accepted. The very essence of trust is necessary, and without it, we miss out on the fullness of life God intends for all people.

Isn't It Ironic—Trust Falls Apart

Ironically, when you set out to convey a value you want people to embody, you witness and experience the challenge in the attribute again and again. For example, when you say, "God, give me patience," it seems there are a number of events that truly test your patience. Or when you say, "God, help me trust again," within days events unfold that cause you to question whether or not you could ever trust people again. For me, a close friend in my life experienced a deep breach in trust in his workplace that led to a negative altercation, which led people to a response out of anger and fear. This experience made me wonder for my friend, who was perceived to be trustworthy, or so he thought, within the organization that he worked for. It made me wonder about what they thought about him and what he thought about them. Were the people he engaged with being authentic and honest? Did they really have faith in his skills and abilities? Did they have any hope that through mediation, conversations, and reconciliation, things could and would change? Or was the tapestry of trust so torn that there was no love left in the relationships he had developed. Since trust goes both ways, it was clear that this particular relationship of trust had no immediate way of being reestablished for the good of both parties. Would they ever be able to find a way to create trust again? This is where the circles of trust are a starting place to finding your own way back to health and wholeness through your relationship with Christ.

Circles of Trust, by Parker Palmer

Where there is a breach of trust, it feels as though it is impossible to go back to the way things were before the breach of trust. Although many people want things to go back to what they experienced when there was high trust, nothing ever stays exactly the same. As time ticks by, things will always change. Parker Palmer's book *A Hidden Wholeness: The Journey toward an Undivided Life* introduces the concept of "circles of trust." Palmer writes, "Wholeness does not mean perfection: it means embracing brokenness as an integral part of life…we can use devastation as a seedbed for new life…the singular intent of a circle of trust: to make it safe for the soul to show up and offer us it's guidance."[1] Although Palmer is talking about the soul, as Christians we may talk about this in terms of the Holy Spirit at work with our whole being to help us heal and find what is needed to move forward into a future with wholeness, living with our creator. Palmer calls this the "inner teacher." Palmer and others acknowledge that we must move with intention and integrity to live into principles that help us be trustworthy. This helps us be clear about what we expect so that we can trust others. Palmer challenges us to think about the kinds of spaces we are good at creating and also the kind of spaces that we know very little about.

> In this culture, we know how to create spaces that invite the intellect to show up, to argue its case, to make its point. We know how to create spaces that invite the emotions to show up, to express anger or joy. We know how to create spaces that invite the will to show up, to consolidate effort and energy round a common task. And we surely know how to create spaces that invite the ego to show up, preening itself and claiming its turf! But we seem to know very little

---

1. Parker Palmer, *A Hidden Wholeness: The Journey toward an Undivided Life* (San Francisco: John Wiley & Sons, 2004), 5, 22.

about creating spaces that invite the soul to show up, this core of ourselves, our selfhood.[2]

Palmer's practices are helpful as we look at ways in which we can move ahead when trust has been broken. He suggests the following practices that can "develop a stronger sense of purpose and integrity," and create a "greater capacity to build the relational trust that helps institutions pursue their missions."[3]

1. Creating spaces that are open and hospitable, but resource-rich and charged with expectancy.

2. Committing to no fixing, advising, "saving" or correcting one another.

3. Asking honest, open questions to "hear each other into speech."

4. Exploring the intersection of the universal stories of human experience with the personal stories of our lives.

5. Using multiple modes of reflection so everyone can find his or her place and pace.

6. Honoring confidentiality.[4]

Let's unpack these practices by using the theological inquiry into evidence of these practices in the Bible:

Old Testament: Circles of Trust

The relationship between Samuel and Eli illustrates a circle of trust between each other and with God. The circle really began when

2. "The Circle of Trust Approach," Center for Courage and Renewal, accessed April 10, 2017, http://www.couragerenewal.org/approach/.
3. "The Circle of Trust Approach," Center for Courage and Renewal, accessed February 4, 2017, http://www.couragerenewal.org/approach/#practices.
4. Ibid.

Hannah, Samuel's mother, dedicated her son to God and trusted him with Eli, the priest, because of her trust in God. From that first act of trust, Samuel was taught to trust God through his relationship with Eli. Eli's first step in building this relationship began with the space. Palmer says one must first "create a space that is open and hospitable, but resource-rich and charged with expectancy." It was not easy for Eli to create this kind of space as a priest who has just received a message of condemnation from God concerning his own offspring. Just before Samuel appears in the story God is disappointed with Eli's sons who have broken God's trust and even Eli's trust in them. God tells Eli that his sons have lost the inheritance of God's blessings through the priestly role, so someone else more trustworthy than his sons will rise up as God's priestly representative.

> The days are coming soon when I will eliminate both your children and the children of your father's household. There won't be an old person left in your family tree. You'll see trouble in my dwelling place, though all will go well for Israel. But there will never be an old person in your family tree. One of your descendants whom I don't eliminate from serving at my altar will cry his eyes out and be full of grief. Any descendants in your household will die by the sword. And what happens to your two sons Hophni and Phinehas will be a sign for you: they will both die on the same day. Then I will establish for myself a trustworthy priest who will act in accordance with my thoughts and desires. I will build a trustworthy household for him, and he will serve before my anointed one forever. (1 Sam 2:31-35)

How fascinating that Eli plays a major role in the establishment of this "trustworthy priest." Eli is responsible for creating the space that is open and hospitable to this child, Samuel. In those days, priestly roles were handed down through generations, but Eli's sons had taken advantage of that open and hospitable space. It didn't stop Eli from continuing to create, even when the space he was providing was no longer for his own flesh and blood. The authors of 1 Samuel want us to recognize the trust that was being established through the child, Samuel. This environment was "resource-rich and charged with expectancy." A young man was called by God in a time and place where the "Lord's word was rare...and visions weren't widely known" (1 Sam 3:1). Eli trusted God, and God was teaching Samuel to lean wholly on God through Eli's trust in the creator.

Eli's trust in God led him to the next practice that Parker Palmer suggests is important for circles of trust. Palmer says that trusting people need to "commit to no fixing, advising, 'saving' or correcting one another."[5] Eli apparently embodied this practice as he received the striking news from Samuel's vision. Samuel shared what God said about Eli and Eli's family, and rather than getting defensive and denying this vision from God, Eli does not fix, advise, or correct Samuel, because he believes that the higher authority made the decision. This behavior establishes Samuel's trust in God because of Eli's trust in God.

After Samuel heard from God, Eli asked him, "'What did he say to you?...Don't hide anything from me. May God deal harshly with you and worse still if you hide from me a single word from everything he said to you.' So Samuel told him everything and hid nothing from him" (1 Sam 3:17-18). This is the third practice that Palmer suggests is necessary as the circle of trust is established and grown. This practice is about being able to ask honest and open questions that help establish and strengthen trust. You'll note that in this examination we see Eli asking the "open and honest questions" of Samuel about God's message. In many ways, this allows Samuel to be heard through his speech, and Eli's acceptance of the responses to his questions helps establish Samuel as a "trustworthy...prophet" (1 Sam 3:20). Eli responded to this critical call to accountability, saying, "He is the Lord, he will do as he pleases" (1 Sam 3:18).

As we study the Bible, we recognize that these stories have a universality about them that helps deepen human experience. Not only do we examine this story of Samuel, Eli, and God as a circle of trust, we also discover that this story has merit in our own lives. We get the feeling that there was true disappointment by God in Eli's parental role as he failed to discipline his children and set a different path for their behaviors and therefore their future. And there was disappointment by Eli in

5. Ibid.

his own children as he tries to reprimand them in 1 Samuel 2:22-25. As these disappointments surface between Samuel and Eli, the frail human relationships with God are part of the practices within the circle of trust. Without establishing this frailty, it may have been difficult for Eli to trust Samuel and Samuel to trust Eli. Samuel was hesitant to tell Eli about the vision, but Eli insisted and responded with resignation and humility because of his trust in God.

The last two practices that Parker Palmer names in the building of circles of trust are "modes of reflection" and "confidentiality." For these practices, we focus on Eli's relationship with God in their own circle of trust. Samuel wasn't the first to deliver this word about Eli's family. In 1 Samuel 2:27, he is invited by another prophet to reflect upon their sins. Whether God reached out to Eli in other ways, the scriptures do not confirm, but we can see that God uses more than one "mode of reflection" to establish the trusting relationship with God's people. With Samuel established as a "trustworthy prophet," we can see how his ability to handle confidentiality strengthened and established his circle of trust with God and Eli. As far as we know, Samuel did not take this vision to the streets. He took it directly to Eli. Due to the confidentiality in that relationship, Samuel came to be known as a trustworthy prophet. We know that circles of trust include one's ability to leave the words with and among the participants in the relationship. When words leave the safety of the relationship, this is when trust begins to disintegrate and the circle is broken.

These patterns in characteristics of trustworthy people and the characteristics of a trustworthy God point to the beauty of God's design. We see how trust is established through faith, hope, and love in the storied relationships of the Bible. We also see how practices and behaviors between the people and God show us how we can establish trust today.

Practice Makes Perfect

Parker Palmer's insights are consistent with the small deposits of information, shared with one another in mutual knowledge, which become the design that withstands the turmoil of broken trust. If there is enough information and knowledge about each other that helps us see one another's humanity, then imagination can be loosened for the sake of the work and for the relationship. Practices in the circles of trust build the high-trust environment where people can bring their whole selves to the task at hand or the relationship of mutuality. Each little string is connected to one another through these tiny hooks.

Ideally, faith communities are designed as practice stations for circles of trust grounded in faith, hope, and love. Christian faith communities are "workout centers" for establishing these circles of trust. Stop for a minute and ask yourself the following questions as a leader in your faith community:

1. Do we create spaces that are open and hospitable, but resource-rich and charged with expectancy?

2. Are we committed to no fixing, advising, "saving" or correcting one another (in ways that establish God as ultimate creator and judge)?[6] Do we ask honest, open questions to "hear each other into speech"?

3. Do we explore the intersection of the universal stories of human experience with the personal stories of our lives (in relation to the scriptures and our understanding of God)?

4. Do we use multiple modes of reflection so everyone can find his or her place and pace?

5. Do we honor confidentiality?[7]

If we lack these practices in our faith communities, then it's hard for guests and participants to venture beyond their first encounter to trust their neighbors, institutions, other people in the world, and ultimately God. The scriptures are always calling us to put our full trust in God. If

---

6. The words in parentheses are my additions to Palmer's practices as I invite you to consider this from a Christian lens.
7. Ibid.

the church as the body of Christ can't practice this trust, where will we learn trust?

One of my favorite illustrations of a faith community that reflected this type of circle of trust was in our Wisconsin Conference Council on Youth Ministries. As a young leader in this environment, I knew I wanted to create a space where young people felt safe, valued, and empowered to "let their souls show up" and their creativity run free. In the four years I served in this ministry, I watched groups of young people embody these practices that developed into a high-trust community that led programs for thousands of youth across the state of Wisconsin. This group of young leaders created a space that was "open, hospitable, resource-rich (with adult leaders willing to listen and learn from youth), and charged with expectancy." The youth in this community knew that they were welcome to share their ideas, and there were no "bad ideas." They were taught to respect one another's thinking and ask one another open and honest questions. The greatest gifts came in faith-sharing moments in which they were invited to tell their stories through the lens of the question, "Where did you see God at work this week?" And as Christian educators, we knew that we had to give them multiple modes of reflection and engagement in order to discover and meet individuals where they were at in their journey toward discovering their "wholeness." Deep in the evenings of a retreat, confidentiality was a must. Students shared with one another and with adult leaders hopes, dreams, fears, and wonders, trusting that those thoughts would be held in deepest confidence. Each group only journeyed one year in this community together, but the circle of trust that they established shaped their faith in God and their faith in humanity throughout their lives. Many of these young leaders have gone on into positions as engineers, doctors, lawyers, and educators who are changing the world. I would like to believe that this community of faith helped deepen their faith, strengthened their hope, and confirmed their love of God and love of neighbor, helping them act as trustworthy leaders and as leaders who trust God.

Layers of Trust

As I noted in the beginning, psychologist Erik Erikson focused on the psycho-social stages of development that help people identify what is needed to develop a strong self-identity that can navigate the joys and challenges of life. As an infant, navigating the realm of trust versus mistrust is critical as one moves into the next stage of development. Sociologists, as they examine the environment and the context where you are living, recognize that there are certain layers of trust that also must be navigated successfully in order to enrich a person's engagement in their communities. These social-psychological concepts are clues to rebuilding broken trust on a healthy foundation.

Do you remember the stories that were told about your infancy? You know, the stories told about the time your brother dropped you on your head, but somehow you survived. For my daughter, one story recalls the time when she was about eight months old, and I was standing next to her in the back of our green Dodge Durango. She seemed to be standing so well, and her diaper bag was just in the back of the SUV, so I thought I would quickly grab it while she was standing there. As I went to grab the bag, little did I know that she thought she should follow me, and out she went tumbling onto the cement on her little head. She screamed at the top of her lungs and at that moment I felt like the least trustworthy mother in the entire world. Or so I thought. Erikson argues that in our first year of life, we are discovering what is a trustworthy experience and who are trustworthy people. Will my environment be consistently safe? Will the adults in my life meet my needs? Will I be protected because I can't protect myself? This is a critical stage of development. An infant first learns to trust his or her parents. These are the people charged with the responsibility of providing for the infant's everyday needs.

If stage one of Erikson's psycho-social development is navigated well and successfully, then your family is the first circle beyond yourself that receives the greatest level of trust for most matters in your life. You trust your family members with your thoughts, your ideas, and your visions because they were there, and if all goes according to plan, they continue to be there as sources of strength and security for your well-being. They have faith in you and your abilities. They hope for your best future, and they often worked and sacrificed for your best future. Your family often loves you the most. This is the ideal situation in which we tend to hope and believe people operate in as they navigate these different layers within the circles of trust.

The next layers of trust are usually institutions built upon the equity of trust. As noted in the previous chapters, educational institutions, health-care institutions, governmental institutions, and faith-based institutions carry our trust because they are necessary for our engagement and flourishing in community. But this layer of trust has been waning and falls prey as the source of much broken trust. When these layers are broken, they can have a great deal of negative effect on our communities. As we have explored through the purposes of faith, hope, and love, I wonder what will be helpful and necessary for us to trust institutions and the leaders in those institutions again? What will it take for us to build trustworthy communities that persist into the future?

As discussed earlier, we are willing to trust complete strangers more than the institutions designed to protect us and help us. With platforms of trust shifting and exchange of trust changing the ways in which we deal with one another, we are discovering that a person's reputation can be strengthened or destroyed through the market layers of trust in the marketplace. If technology changes this layer of trust, then we acknowledge that technology can affect the institutional layer and the family layer of trust as well.

Technology changes the way institutions present their beliefs, their values, and their ideologies. In the current political landscape, leading politicians use Twitter to communicate their stance. For better or worse, this creates a whole new challenge when we are trying to establish trust for the institutions they lead. Faith institutions and government institutions battle for space in the distracted eyes of the readers as they make declarations for and against each other. They create viral and toxic groundswells of indignation, calls for justice, and even appeals for hate.

In 140 characters or less, people are prompted for action, and millions of people can be motivated to come together in hundreds of cities across the globe through the rapid spread of information.[8] If institutions aren't careful about how they wield their power on technology platforms, they can and will make or break trust in ways we have never even imagined.

Technology also changes the family layer of trust. If you aren't lucky enough to be in the most inner circles of some families, then in today's world you will likely discover new pregnancies, new relationships, and even new life statuses on Twitter or Facebook. From gender reveals to "we're expecting" photos, technology shifts how we discover information about our own families. There is nothing more telling about your proximity to someone's layers of trust than the status of Facebook. If you are really close to a family member or friend and they deeply trust you with information, then you will at least receive a phone call or be told in person about an important event in their life. But if you are not in the closest layer of trust, your information medium may be like the hundreds or thousands of other friends who will receive the news via a change in status or a photo posted on Facebook, Twitter, or Instagram. Some family and friends may be deeply insulted, while others see this shift in platform as a norm. And just like the institutional layer of trust, technology can enhance or destroy the family layer of trust with the tap of a finger.

Technology can help a "market layer" of trust to thrive. Botsman reminds us that the layers of trust in the marketplace have drastically shifted in the digital era:

> We are inventing a type of trust that can grease the wheels of business and facilitate person-to-person relationships in the age of distributed networks and collaborative marketplaces. A type of trust that transforms the social glue for ideas whether it be for renting your house to someone you don't know, making a loan to unknown borrowers on a social lending platform, and getting in a car with

---

8. The women's march on January 21, 2017, unified people across cities around the world standing up for justice for women and equal rights for all.

a stranger from being considered personally risky, to the building blocks of multi-billion dollar businesses.[9]

When we buy online from eBay or Amazon or hundreds of other stores, or when we use phone apps to secure a ride, we use layers of trust in the marketplace with regularity. We trust this market layer more than the institutional circle of trust because of "the trust stack."[10] Because the marketplace finds way to equalize the customer and the provider through rating systems, we trust the ratings of other strangers. The more strangers rate the provider, the more confidence we have. And if the distributor guarantees a refund, we add another layer. The trust exchange shifts as collaborative consumption[11] changes the culture of doing business. Trust can be deepened or destroyed through technology just like the other drivers of trust.

Jon Ronson is a writer and journalist who wrote the book *So You've Been Publicly Shamed.* On a TED Radio interview on September 8, 2015, he revealed stories that examined Twitter users who showed their dissatisfaction with a company or service and then were publicly shamed by their insensitivity. For example, a woman on the train in Philadelphia immediately after a crash tweeted out, "Thanks a lot for derailing my train. Can I please get my violin back from the second car of the train?"[12] Little did she know that two hundred people were injured in that wreck and eight people lost their lives. In response, social media strangers jumped on her and branded her as insensitive, self-centered, and whiny. Her name was plastered all over social media, and her reputation as an individual human being plummeted. Ronson said, "She

9. Rachel Botsman, "The Changing Rules of Trust in the Digital Age," *Harvard Business Review,* October 20, 2015, https://hbr.org/2015/10/the-changing-rules-of-trust-in-the-digital-age.

10. Described in previous chapters as the way in which people come to trust strangers.

11. A term coined by Botsman as she expands trust research.

12. "How Can Our Real Lives Be Ruined by Our Digital Ones?" NPR: TED Radio Hour, September 18, 2015, http://www.npr.org/templates/transcript/transcript.php?storyId=440286008.

was threatened and harassed and had to go into hiding."[13] Technology changed her nonchalant comment on Twitter into a major breach of trust as an insensitive human being. As Ronson points out, this story and others like it have changed the social conventions that foster trust.

The furthest or outer layer of trust in our relationships is the society in general.[14] These are the strangers. They are the neighbors who live in your town but you never really know. They are the people in your geographical boundary or the citizens of the world. They are so different from you, and yet they can be so similar to you, and sometimes you extend them trust and sometimes they extend you trust without ever knowing their name. In the "society layer" we exchange trust with people and draw conclusions about our societies based upon the exchange of trust. Technology also drastically shifts how our societies exchange trust.

If we examine trust throughout different countries and cultures, we find variation that depends on access to the Internet. Another example of how social levels of trust have shifted because of technology is the 2016 US elections. Accusations from both candidates drew suspicion about how social media was being used to manipulate the results. Many communities questioned whether or not the outcomes based upon the available technology used were reliable. They questioned whether or not other countries were tampering with the election process, and they questioned whether or not groups were maliciously leaking information to discredit one candidate or the other. Trust at the society level is and has been breached and entangled. Some would argue that social media in particular is the primary culprit for a social bankruptcy in trust.

This demonstrates that there is no shortage of broken trust by individuals, institutions, and society itself. What can faith, hope, and love do to change the outcomes of broken trust? What is the responsibility of faith communities as they seek to change behaviors through loving God and loving neighbor?

---

13. Ibid.

14. Stephanie Olexa, "The 5 Circles of Trust," Lead to the Future, accessed May 10, 2017, http://www.leadtothefuture.com/the-5-circles-of-trust/.

Curiousity about Trust

My curiosity about trust is not yet completely satisfied. I still ponder how trust can be strengthened, enhanced, and developed so that faith communities can find their way back into the mainstream of influencing the cultures and societies where we have been planted. So I sent out a survey utilizing social media to reach colleagues in faith communities. I asked them and their networks to identify the characteristics and behaviors that help leaders establish trust through the Christian faith that God could be proud of. The survey itself was an exercise in trust. I was somewhat surprised by the response rate.

Survey on Trust

First, leaders are less inclined to fill out a survey about trust because they are suspicious about the motivation and rationale for doing this kind of survey. A colleague was hesitant to send it to her constituents because they might think she doesn't trust them. Others weren't sure they trusted that the survey would remain anonymous or that someone might use their responses against them. I sent a similar research survey about "generativity" to the same network and received over three hundred responses. On the trust survey there were just over one hundred respondents from a potential sample of over thirteen hundred people. The generativity survey brought in responses from 23 percent of the people surveyed. The trust survey had 8 percent of the potential audience responding. And out of that 8 percent nearly 40 percent skipped the last questions about characteristics of trust that they saw in themselves. It makes me wonder even more why church leaders are so hesitant to engage the idea of trust and even more afraid to claim that they themselves are and can be trustworthy leaders.

If we are honest with ourselves, most leaders in the church are constantly questioning themselves as they examine their own abilities to lead others in the relational practices of faith, hope, and love. As Craig Hill points out in his book about ambition,[15] we waffle between being confident in our call and being humbled by our call. Should we stand in pride of our ability to lead in the church, or should we fall prostrate to the God who called us into these roles?

A large majority of the participants were forty-five years and older and 75 percent of the respondents were female. Almost everyone identified themselves as currently an active participant in a church or faith-based institution. A majority are members in congregations but not clergy or lay leaders in their church/faith-based settings. And 80 percent of the respondents identify themselves as "mainline Protestants." Even though a survey didn't entice more people to respond about their ideas concerning trust, it did provide anecdotal evidence to consider.

When asked about the most important characteristics of someone you trust, the top three were honesty, integrity, and respect, in that order. When asked about the most important characteristics of church leaders, they chose integrity, honesty, and care in that order. When asked about characteristics essential for building a high-trust culture, they selected honesty, love, and respect as the top three. And when asked about what would be necessary for one to feel as though they could take risks, the top three selections were integrity, honesty, and respect, with competence not far behind. Creative and innovative environments need honesty, respect, and love.

There seems to be a deep desire and need for honest people who have integrity, show respect, and demonstrate care and love through their leadership roles. If these core characteristics are a part of their environments, then they can be creative, be innovative, take risks, and help create high-trust cultures. This response reinforces our claim that through faith in one another, hope for our future, and love for our neighbors, ourselves, and our communities, we can build high-trust cultures that allow for creativity and innovation to emerge. These high-trust cultures can be created, practiced, and perfected in our faith communities. Faith communities and churches across our world can and

15. Craig C. Hill, *Servant of All: Status, Ambition, and the Way of Jesus* (Grand Rapids: Wm. B. Eerdmans, 2016), 31.

should be trust training centers where we are challenged, equipped, and prepared to change the world as Christians who trust God, trust others, and are deemed trustworthy. And like any physical training center, when we fall, or lose, or are lost, then the training center is there to help us get back up again, aim for a new path, and get back to where we can train and be trained all over again.

By a wide margin the respondents didn't feel their faith community has a high-trust culture. In fact, most of the respondents said that "too many members' attitudes make it difficult to have a high-trust culture." We have a long road ahead if we are to become trust training centers equipping people to live into God's vision for our world. If God designed creation to trust God, trust self, and trust neighbors, then the first place these exercises in trust must start is within the body of Christ. We must live into being the centers of faith where we leap into trust because of God's invitation to each and every one of us. We must become beacons of hope that constantly remind people that we can trust God to carry us through both wonderful and joyous moments as well as the moments that cause us to explore the *dark night of our souls.*[16] We must witness and embody Christ's love for all people, whether Jew or Greek, slave or free, so that people can experience and discover what trusting God looks like and feels like. Love of God and love of neighbor leads us to trust God and trust neighbor, no matter how deep they are in our layers of trust.

High-Trust Culture Essential in the Church

The church should be one of the primary training centers in building high-trust communities and high-trust cultures. Our faith in Jesus requires trust. Just as secular environments advocate for high-trust cultures in the workplace, in institutions, and in the marketplace, the church should and must be one of the primary places where people can

---

16. The title of a poem written by Saint John of the Cross.

learn to trust, exercise trust, and become trustworthy because we trust God and God trusts us as partners in relieving human suffering.

The Christian church bears a great responsibility for building trust. We have a great responsibility to take risks that reinforce our trust in God. If we live in fear from broken trust, then we miss the wholeness of God's vision for us and God's vision for the world. In high-trust cultures, barriers are broken and walls come crumbling down. In high-trust cultures, people step across lines of division and become beacons of hope and life to those who are weary of trust. And when trust is broken by neighbors, faithful people rise up again because their whole trust is in God.

Confession Helps Honesty

Parker Palmer explains that wholeness in life is discovered when we can be honest with ourselves. When being honest with one's self, sometimes it's best to start with confession. Therefore, I confess that the current state of the country where I live is in disarray, in my opinion. I confess that the Christian denomination where I belong is deeply struggling with trust issues. I confess that my closest friends and family are broken by issues of lost trust. And I confess that there are days when I don't really trust my own thinking about my words in this book. But at the end of the day, I trust God. I put my whole trust in God's love and grace. I lean wholly not on my own understanding but on God, "for the foolishness of God is wiser than human wisdom, and the weakness of God is stronger than human strength" (1 Cor 1:18-31). I put my whole trust in God's ability to help us find the good in the midst of human tragedy, and I wholeheartedly trust God's understanding and humbly acknowledge my limitations to grasping that understanding.

In light of these confessions and the search for honesty, what would a "trust training center" look like in our faith communities today? Trust training centers would be grounded in the practices of faith, hope, and love. They would excel in teaching people what faith looks like in our world today. Out of these foundations, we would practice honesty in all things, including with ourselves, finding ways to allow our souls to show up. As Parker Palmer illustrates through trust circles, we become whole when allowing our souls to show up, free and transparently honest. The wholeness of one's self gives us the freedom to explore the depths of our understanding. Being honest with one's self and finding wholeness gives us the freedom to appreciate our differences.

Alexa[17] and I were in conversation about the human sexuality differences in our church. We were struggling with whether or not the people proclaiming such distinct positions in the church could honestly be members of the same denomination. Since both of us traveled in circles that were different from our own beliefs, we found ourselves opening up about how we had withheld our opinions for fear of offending people in those circles who didn't know us or would have judged us had they known our stance. Sadly, neither of us felt that we could safely be honest with the people we were working with because we didn't trust that they would respect us if they knew what we really thought.

When a church is a trust training center, it allows people to be honest with their fears, their beliefs, and their questions. We can't silence people because of our judgments and frighten or judge people's souls back into hiding because we are unwilling to hear how their beliefs, attitudes, and understandings about life might be different than our own. Broken trust often stems from fear of our own truths. If we are honest with ourselves and with the people in our churches, we can engage in a conversation about truth that allows us to wrestle with what truth means for one person over the other. By wrestling with this together, we may discover the truth that the Holy Spirit needs us to see in order to grow closer to Christ through our honest engagement with our neighbors.

---

17. Name changed to protect identity.

The Church: Trust Training Centers

If honesty, integrity, and respect were built, practiced, and strengthened in every aspect of the church's life, we would experience the core practices needed for repairing broken trust in our world. These three characteristics can be lived out and exercised every day among leaders in the denomination to leaders in seminaries to leaders in the congregation. If leaders in the church could be honest about their fears, their disappointments, their passions and desires, then they can live with integrity for other Christians in our communities of faith. You might be thinking, *I can't be completely honest about all these things because the people in my church will judge me and they will no longer follow me if they knew that this is the way I feel about* _____. However, if you are hiding it, then you are not living whole. And how can we trust our leaders if they, too, are not living whole as God intends?

Having worked with youth and young adults for a large portion of my ministry, I know that they can see through hidden brokenness quicker than I can see it myself. Youth can tell when you are holding something back, and they will find a way to draw the truth if not the clarity out of you. Perhaps this perspicuity among youth is why I am blatantly honest with my thoughts, my ideas, and even my Pollyannaish ideals. I discovered that this transparency wasn't acceptable in the polite politics of the church. I learned that sharing too much information might lead to people using that information through political tactics that I was too naïve to understand.

Sadly, the trust levels in the church world are very low, which makes my soul retreat and my level of trust diminish. It will take years of hard work to build back the levels of trust that inhabit a flourishing church.

Living with integrity for me means finding ways to allow my soul to trust again even when I fear that my trust will be broken. Living with this kind of integrity means setting aside the history of my experiences and hoping for people to rise to the expectations of a high-trust culture, even when they have fallen short. Some people may call it crazy, and others would carefully guard their hearts and souls when trust has been broken, but our God calls us to live a different life. God reaches out to trust humanity time and time again, even after generation after generation has broken God's trust. We've got to live a life worthy of God's trust through our faithfulness with each other. Hanging in the balance is our hope for the world and our love for all.

The Beautiful Tapestry of Trust

When trust is at its best in our world, it is beautiful. Like the art at the Crystal Bridges Art Museum in Arkansas, it is woven together through so many small hooks and millions and millions of multicolored threads that it will capture your imagination for hours and hours on end. Consider the possibilities if we hook ourselves into God's design.

I was on my way to the Philippines on an Asian airline and there were two commercials that kept airing before every movie. One commercial was of a young man and a young woman at the lake enjoying the glorious full moon when he looks down at his watch and discovers the time. He jumps up and rushes to an elderly fisherman on a bike. He begs him for the bike and trades his watch for the bike. He props the young woman on the back of the bike and takes off. He bikes up a tedious hill and crosses a rickety old bridge. They are followed by a yelping dog, and he quickly pedals right up to an aqua-green cottage with a white picket fence. He leans the bike on the side of the fence, grabs the young woman's hand, and goes to the front door. The door opens and her father stands there as she waves goodbye. He looks at his watch and the long hand reaches the top, indicating he made curfew at 11:00 p.m. He smiles awkwardly at the father, and the father smiles his approval and closes the door. The young man collapses on the ground, exhausted by the trek but satisfied that he earned the trust of the young woman and her father. At the end the words go up, "Trust is a one-time gift."[18]

Although life is much easier if we build trust from the beginning of our relationships, it isn't just a one-time gift when it comes to understanding faith. It is strengthened and enhanced by those momentary

---

18. United Overseas Bank, "UOB Private Bank 'Bicycle' TV Commercial," YouTube, May 31, 2016, https://youtu.be/ZGYcHixmZhs.

actions that build the trust design, but stories like these help us appreciate how critical, beautiful, and fragile this gift of trust can be in our world today. My desire is that you'll see what your role is in God's beautiful tapestry of trust. Our hope is that you'll see the church's role as a training center for trust. And you'll continue to discover how trust in God creates the foundations for trust in ourselves and trust in our neighbors. Let's keep discovering God's trust together.

CPSIA information can be obtained
at www.ICGtesting.com
Printed in the USA
LVOW13s2038040817
543760LV00001B/1/P